Occupations

A Preliminary List

SECOND EDITION

Joyce Culling

Federation of Family History Societies

Published by
The Federation of Family History Societies (Publications) Ltd
2-4 Killer Street, Ramsbottom, Bury
Lancashire BL0 9BZ

First published 1994
Second edition 1999

ISBN 1-86006 103 6

Printed and bound by Oxiniprint
Great Clarendon Street, Oxford OX2 6DP

Contents

Long Song Seller

Introduction

Occupation, Trade, Rank or Profession

Under this heading in 19th century Census Returns can be found some of the most revealing clues to family history. The occupation of the head of the household determined the life style of the family, dictating how and where they lived. Frequently it affected the next generations as sons followed their fathers occupations or carried on the family business, while marriage often strengthened ties between families already connected by trade or occupation.

There are several thousand occupations listed in Census Return Tables with many sub-divisions noted in manufacturing areas. While some terms are vague and of doubtful interpretation the great majority are self explanatory or are easily identified. However, in some instances, a specific occupation can be known by different names, or the same name is applied to very different trades, depending on the locality.

Although people designated their own occupations on the household schedules the census enumerators were given official guidelines to establish specific classifications. Thus 'servant' had to be identified as 'domestic' or 'indoor' from 1881, and we can be truly grateful to the diligent enumerator who added 'railway' or 'factory' to the vague term 'engineer'.

In some records a human tendency to upgrade one's own occupation or that of an ancestor can be misleading, as can the description of two female servants, given in a Liverpool census return, 'Kept by the Flour Dealer'. Other colourful 'occupations' which have been noted include, 'A life long interest in money', 'Cook in a Big House', 'Keeps a Mangle', 'Fear-Nothing-Maker', or one that at first glance would seem to refer to place of birth ' A Scotsman'.

There are many instances of people having two occupations, and apart from soldiers and sailors with civilian trades, the most commonly noted are complementary, e.g. auctioneer and valuer, carpenter and joiner, chemist and druggist, glazier and glass maker, printer and publisher. Some associations are traditional, like the apothecary and grocer (the 13th century spicers who sold spices for medicinal purposes were the forerunners of the apothecary and pharmacist), or the plumber and glazier (being a worker in lead one of the plumbers original jobs was to fix the glass in windows, hence lead lighting). There are also several instances of two apparently unconnected trades carried on at the same time by the same person, such as gardener and barber, cord-wainer and publisher, coal agent and blacksmith, smith and cow-leech, farmer and weaver. Many dual occupations were seasonal, the farm worker following the barley harvest to work in the brewery for the winter. The Bass Brewery in Stoke employed most of the men from several East Anglian villages in this way. A seasonal job could of course be missed from a census return but delving into the local history of an area should provide such information.

Parish records, Poll books, wills, trade directories, and birth, marriage and death certificates can also provide interesting facts about the working life of our ancestors. Many occupations have been overtaken by machinery and technology and no longer exist, some like that of barker or chaucer are remembered only in our surnames. Old documents are often difficult to decipher because of condition or unfamiliar script, but archaic spelling and dialect give rise to most problems in identifying occupations.

Some Useful Sources

Any good dictionary can be consulted for meanings of the more commonly known occupations, but for the sheer volume of quotes from obsolete technical sources the original New Oxford English Dictionary provides invaluable help, as does Wright's English Dialect Dictionary and any local dialect publication for a particular area.

Information about twentieth century occupations can be found in "Classification of Occupations and Directory of Occupational Titles", published by H.M.S.O. and regularly updated.

Most Record Offices will have copies of the official Government Reports, published after each census was taken, "Population Tables of England and Wales, Census of Great Britain". These include various statistics and information relating to trades and occupations which can be most helpful to the family historian. For example, 1851 statistics linking population movement and occupations show that people moved frequently and freely, some- times only a short distance. As in Derbyshire, where an increase in population in Litchurch since the 1841 census was ascribed to the extension of silk and lace manufactories in the adjoining town of Derby. Migration of workers due to stoppage of mills, in the Darley Abbey district, was given as the reason for a decrease in the population.

Victoria County Histories contain useful background information on local industry and large estates, perhaps revealing unsuspected connections with other counties which may account for a move by a family. Local Authority archives may contain lists of freemen and apprentices or provide detailed information about trade and industry in the area. Trade directories, newspapers and contemporary maps may also provide further clues to local occupations, as do the many 'Working Museums' now in existence.

There are many books available which deal with specific trades and occupations and those listed in the bibliography proved to be a rich and sometimes the only source of information on the more unusual, obscure or obsolete ones, as well as the more familiar.

This revised list of occupations includes over five hundred which have been collected since the 'Preliminary List' was published. I have appreciated the correspondence this has prompted and to havehelped with some queries. Thanks must go to my husband Harold Culling for typing in all the additions on an ageing and ailing computer, and to Bob Boyd who has brought this edition to life.

Any dates and places given refer to one specific usage and locality whenever and wherever this has been determined. Any additions to this list would be appreciated.

> "All society would appear to arrange
> itself into four different classes,
> 1. Those that will work
> 2. Those that cannot work
> 3. Those that will not work
> 4. Those that need not work."

(Henry Mayhew *London Labour and the London Poor,* 1861)

Glossary

Abbreviations used

A/S	Anglo Saxon
coll.	colloquial
dial.	dialect
Fr.	French
Mil.	Military
Naut.	Nautical
orig.	originally

The following Chapman County Codes are used for places

CON	Cornwall	SAL	Salop
CUL	Cumberland	SCT	Scotland
DBY	Derbyshire	SFK	Suffolk
HUN	Huntingdonshire	SOM	Somerset
LAN	Lancashire	SSX	Sussex
LON	London	STS	Staffordshire
NBL	Northumberland	YKS	Yorkshire
NFK	Norfolk	WES	Westmorland

A Peddler

Occupations List

ABSORBER MAN Worker in chemical plant responsible for a specific process.

ABLE SEAMAN A Seaman who reaches a certain standard of technical skill above that of the Ordinary Seaman.

ABTHANE A Steward. Old Title of the High Steward of Scotland.

ACATER Ships Chandler. (from Fr. achateur buyer)

ACCIPITRARY A falconer.

ACCOMPTANT Accountant.

ACTIONER Skilled craftsman specialising in the firing mechanisms of gunmaking.

ACTION-FILER In piano making one responsible for preparing the metal action parts for nickel plating.

ACKERMAN Acreman, Ploughman. Oxherd 18c.

ADVERTISEMENT CONVEYANCER Sandwich Board Man. Term coined by Gladstone.

ADZER Woodworker who rough cut solid chair bases with an adze for the chair maker.

AERONAUT 19c. A trapeze artist in a circus. A balloonist.

AIGRETTE MAKER One who made small feather plumes for certain articles of dress, a plumette maker.

AGWALLA An Asiatic ship's fireman.

ALCHER Worker who tied up hanks of hosiery or wool into convenient bundles.

ALE-CONNER Official who tested the quality of ale and measures in public houses. An Ale-Taster (q.v.)

ALE-DRAPER Ale seller, publican, innkeeper.

ALE-FOUNDER see Ale-Conner.

ALESTAN(D) BEARER A pot boy in an inn.

ALE-TASTER An inspector of ale. Appointed by manor or vestry he proclaimed the permitted price for selling beer & ale. When brewers wished him to call an ale-stake or pole was placed, or held by a pot boy, in front of the ale-house.

ALE-TUNNER Brewery worker who filled tuns or casks with ale.

ALE-WIFE A woman who kept an ale-house.

ALL-SPICE A 19c. grocer.

ALLEY-GIRL Worker in soap manufactury who inspected tablets of soap leaving the stamping machine.

ALLSORTS STRIPPER Sugar confectionery worker who prepared the liquorice for rolling and cutting.

ALMANAC MAN A Lincolnshire official responsible for warning inhabitants near the Trent river of expected high tides.

ALMATOUR An Almoner.

ALMSMAN One who received support by alms.

ALNAGER 16c-18c. A sworn official appointed to examine and attest the quality of woollen goods sold in a port or market town, stamping approved cloth with the town seal.

AMBLER An officer of the Royal Stable, who broke in horses. i.e. taught them to amble.

ANCHORESS 15c/16c. A hermit, a woman who retired from society to become a religious recluse.

ANCHORITE See above. Refers to a male.

ANCILLE A maid servant.

ANIMAL & BIRD PRESERVER 19c. Taxidermist.

ANGLE IRON SMITH Metal worker who made angle iron (Flat iron bar, bent at right angles longitudinally).

ANKERMAN See Anchoress. Servant of a religious recluse.

ANKLE BEATER A young boy who assisted drover in driving cattle to market.

ANNATTO MAKER One who worked in the manufacture of colour dyes for paint, printing etc.

ANNEALER Tin plate worker.

ANNUITANT Person in receipt of, or who has entitlement to receive, an annuity, a pensioner.

ANTIGROPELOS MAKER Shoemaker who made waterproof leggings.

APOTHECARY Chemist or Druggist.

APPRAISER Broker of household goods.

APPRENTICE Learner of craft, bound to serve & entitled to instruction from his employer for a specific term.

APRONEER 17/18c London. Shopkeeper. Apron Man.

APPROVER Official responsible for the renting of the King's desmesnes in small manors.

ARCHIATOR A physician.

ARCHIL MAKER One who made Archil, a violet dye produced from lichen, used in manufacture of wall washes, in textile industry, etc.

ARCUBALISTER A crossbow man

ARGOLET A light horseman.

ARKWRIGHT Skilled craftsman who specialised in making arks, i.e. wooden chests or coffers with domed lids.

ARRAYER An Army officer, who had charge of the soldier's armour.

ARMOURER Maker of armour.

ARTICULATOR (of bones and skeletons) One who assembles same for display purposes.

ARTIST-in-FIREWORKS. 1830 Birmingham. Person who prepared and presented firework displays for festive occasions.

ASHBANK FAIRY Labourer who removed waste ashes from ashpits, and tipped them onto an ash dump.

ASHMAN Dustman, rubbish collector; see Nightman.

ASSAYER Taster of food in noble or royal households to guard against poisoning.

AWAITER Attendant.

AXE-PEDDLAR Dealer in ashes, a hawker of wood ash.

AXEWADDLER Dealer in ashes(DEV) see Ax-peddlar.

AXLETREE TURNER Maker of axles for wheels.

BABBITER Metal processor working in white metal used to line bearings.

BABY FARMER A foster mother or nurse performing the duties of a parent to the child of another for payment.

BACK-END MAN Operator of fabric stretching machine in textile mill. Also Stenterer and Tenterer.

BACKMAKER Cooper who made 'Backs', tubs & vats as used in baking, brewing, dyeing, laundry.

BACKSTER/BAXTER Originally female baker, by 18c. term referred to both sexes

BACK'US BOY A 'back-of-the-house' boy, a kitchen servant employed in a farmhouse.

BACK WASHER Cleanser of wool (worsted manufacture).

BADGER 1. Pauper who was obliged to wear badge bearing letter 'P' under Condition of Settlement Act 1697, 2. Itinerant trader, usually dealing in food, 3. Corn dealer or miller, 4. Small shopkeeper(LAN) 5. Etcher of decorative glassware. See also Cadger, Hawker, Higgler, Peddar.

BADGY FIDDLER 1850 1900. A boy trumpeter. Military coll.

BAGBEATER Labourer in cement works who cleaned sacks by beating with a stick to remove cement particles.

BAGMAN 18c Commercial Traveller, so called because samples were originally carried in saddle bags.

BAILIFF(BAILIE) An officer of the sheriff, having power of arrest. A land steward.

BAIRMAN/BAREMAN A Pauper.

BALLAD MONGER A street seller of printed ballads.

BALDERER Stone breaker working on road construction and repairs.

BALLAST HEAVER 19c. Dock-worker who laid heavy matter in the empty hold of a ship to keep it steady.

BALLER Cotton or silk worker who winds thread into balls.

BALLER-UP Assisted the pottery thrower, weighing out balls of clay.

BALLY Metal worker who works at a ball furnace which produces a pure form of wrought iron.

BAL-MAIDEN 19c.CON. (Bal = mine) Female worker employed above ground in various processes of dressing tin and copper ores. See Pit-Brow Lass.

BANDADY/BHANDARY An Asiatic ship's cook specially qualified for preparing dishes for the Asiatic crew members.

BAND-FILER Metal worker in gun making trade.

BANDSTER One who bound the sheaves after reaping.

BANG-BEGGAR A parish officer responsible for controlling the stay of any stranger. Sometimes the local constable or Beadle.

BANG-STRAW 18c. A thresher, sometimes any outdoor farm servant.

BANKER/BANKSMAN A ditcher, one who dug trenches to facilitate drainage of land, and carried out repairs.

BANKSMAN A colliery worker in charge of the cages at pit top. Also known as Bank Manager.

BANK TENDER See Banker.

BANK WALKER Patrols canal and river banks and waterworks channels. Gives instructions to Bankers(q.v.) as to necessary repairs.

BANT MAKER Weaver of narrow band and webbing.

BARBER-SURGEON Until 1745 barbers were also surgeons. The Company of Barber-Surgeons was incorporated 1461, and barbers were allowed to practise in surgery and dentistry until 16c. when an Act of Parliament restricted barbers to dentistry and the Company title was altered to 'Barbers AND Surgeons'. An Act of 1745 allowed surgeons their own Corporation but the name persisted until 19c. Traditionally Surgeons still take the title "Mister" because of the historical association.

BARGAIN LETTER Manager of slate quarry. Sets prices of rock for sale or letting .

BARKEEPER One who kept guard at a tollbar, barrier or gate to prevent passage until the appropriate toll was paid.

BARGE-MATE Naval 19c. Officer who was in charge of a ship while a visit by notabilities was taking place.

BARKER/BARKMAN Tanner of leather. Originally one who stripped trees of bark for use in the process of tanning.

BARMASTER Authority to whom all disputes in lead mining industry was referred. Also in charge of standard measure used in mining of ore.

BARREL-FILER Worker involved in gun-making.

BARROWMAN Coal pit worker, brought coal from the face to the foot of the shaft.

BASKETMAN Rural craftsman who used plaited willow twigs to make various receptacles as well as chairs, cradles etc.

BATER Leather dresser.

BATTER Woman employed in cleaning raw cotton by beating it with a bat, operation later done by machinery.(LAN)

BAYWEAVER Weaver of bay, a fine light woollen fabric. Its manufacture was introduced to England in 16c. by fugitives from France & Netherlands. Often corrupted to 'baize'.

BEADLE A parish officer with duties varying in each locality, such as assistant to the constable, town crier, messenger.

BEAD(S)MAN 1. One who prayed for others i.e. one paid to pray for the soul of his benefactor (from rosary beads), 2. Inhabitant of a bedehouse, an almshouse or hospital, 3. Tenant obligated to lord of the manor for a specific service or bede. Hence bedemad (mowing service), 4. A Beadle (q.v.)

BEAMER Textile worker who wound the warp on the roller prior to it being put on the weaving loom.

BEAN MAN Worker in oil manufactury attending the conveyor belt carrying castor oil seed.

BEARER Underground worker in coal mine who carried coal out to the pit bottom, and filled the containers sent up to the surface. Work usually done by women and children before 1846.

BEARWARD Keeper of a Bear.

BEASTMAN see Byreman.

BEATER Fuller. In charge of machine which disintegrates and softens materials.

BEATER-UP Tobacco machine packer.

BEAVER Feltmaker.

BEDDER/BEDDINER An upholsterer (West Country).

BEDMAN A West Country term for a sexton.

BEDWEVERE 1. 14c. NFK. A weaver of bed quilts, 2. Maker of bed-frame webbing.

BEEMASTER Keeper of bees

BEESKEPMAKER Bee hive maker, "Beeskeepmaker".

BEETLEMAKER Maker of wooden paddle used in laundering clothes.

BEETLER One who operated a beetling machine, used to emboss fabric. (Textile Industry)

BEETLERS ODDER Beetlers assistant.

BELLFOUNDER Maker of bells church, cattle, etc.

BELLMAN 1. 17c. Watchman. One of his duties was to bless the sleepers in houses he passed, 2. 18c. Employee of the Post Office who collected letters before the Mail Coach departed at night. He walked the streets ringing a bell, carrying a locked bag with a posting slot. Also known as a Walking Pillar-Box. (service discontinued 1846)

BELLOWFARMER 16/17c. Man responsible for the maintenance of church organs and regals, small portable ones.

BELLY BUILDER Assembler and fitter of piano interiors.

BELTER see Billiter. A Bellfounder.

BERRIER 16c YKS. A thresher.

BESSWARDEN An officer appointed by the parish to look after its beasts.

BESOM MAKER 18c DBY. Broommaker.

BIGGAR A builder.

BILLIARD MARKER Employed in a gentlemen's club, hotel or billiard hall to regulate the game of billiards, keep score, and hold stakes if wagers were made, even after marking boards were in use. At the turn of the century many large houses had their own billiard room and a manservant was often designated as a marker.

BILLIER Bolton LAN 1830. Operator of the Billy Roller, a heavy roving machine used in the manufacture of cotton. Children who handled the Billy were often killed or maimed. The process it performed (slubbing) was eventually incorporated into other machinery. By 1840 the Billy was no longer used. See Slubber.

BILLITER Bellfounder. From billet, an ingot of metal used to cast bells.

BILLMAN 1.Formerly a soldier armed with a bill, a type of pike. 2.A man who cut and sold faggots.

BILLPOSTER/STICKER Pastes posters for advertising purposes on hoardings or other display stations.

BILLYMAN see Billier.

BINDER Employed in various trades such as hatting, bookmaking, shoemaking.

BIRD BOY One employed to scare birds away from growing crops. Also known as a Crowkeeper in some places.

BIRDS NEST SELLER A street seller of wild birds' nests, complete with eggs. These were placed under canaries or bantam-fowl for hatching, to be reared as pets.

BLACK BORDERER In paper making trade worker who made black edged mourning stationery.

BLACK-COAT A Clergyman.

BLACK DYER Specialised feather dyer.

BLACKER A japanner who applies black lacquer to ironware.

BLACK-GUARD Nickname given to the lowest drudges of the Court, carriers of coal and wood, labourers in the scullery etc.

BLACKING MAKER Maker of black substance used for blackening and polishing footware.

BLACK ORNAMENT MAKER/ WORKER A gem cutter who made jet ornaments and jewellery.

BLACK TRAY/WAITER MAKER Maker of Japanned tea trays and salvers.

BLADESMITH A Swordmaker, or cutler.

BLADIER An engrosser of corn.

BLAXTER 17c NFK. Bleacher of cloth.

BLEACHER One who bleached or whitened cloth by exposure to sun or chemicals.

BLEYSTARE A bleacher.

BLINDSMAN Post Office worker who dealt with improperly addressed letters. ca. 1860.

BLOCKCUTTER/BLOCKER A maker of wooden blocks for shaping hats.

BLOCK MAKER A maker of engraved wooden blocks used in printing.

BLO(W)MAN A trumpeter.

BLOODMAN A blood letter.

BLOODLETTER A barber-surgeon. (q.v.) The letting of blood by opening a vein or the application of leeches was a common remedy for all manner of complaints.

BLOOMER A worker at a bloomery, or bloom smithy, a smelter of iron.

BLOWER 1. A man who worked bellows in smelting house of an iron works, 2. Operator of blowing machine which cleansed and separated fibres, in textile and hat making industries, 3. A glass blower.

BLOWFEEDER Worker who fed blowing machine with material. See Blower.

BLUE-MAKER A manufacturer of blue dye used by calico printers. It was also used in laundries and in the domestic wash for 'whitening' linen.

BLUE-MILL-MAN Worker responsible for weighing and mixing the ingredients of laundry blue.

BLUE MANGLER Textile worker operating machine which passed bleached cotton or yarn through laundry blue solution.

BLUFFER 18c. LND Landlord of an inn.

BLUNGER Pottery worker in charge of clay mixing machine.

BLUNT WORKER Maker of steel surgical instruments which do not have a cutting edge.

BOARDER Operator of knitware machine fixing permanent shape of hose or other knitted garments.

BOARDMAN 1. 19/20c. School attendance inspector employed by local School Board, 2. Tenant of land which lord of the manor kept expressly for maintenance of his table, rentals being paid in kind. (Hence bed & board).

BOARDWRIGHT A Carpenter, maker of tables & chairs. See Boardman.

BOATMAN Usually referred to one who worked solely on the boats of inland waterways. See Waterman, Flatman.

BOBBER 1. Polisher of metals, 2. Unloader of fishing vessels.

BOBBIN CARRIER Worker in spinning or weaving mills. Job frequently done by children.

BOBBY 19c.(slang) A Policeman. After Sir Robert Peel, founder of the first police force in 1829. (Also Peeler).

BODEYS/BODY MAKER A Bodice maker. Bodice, a stiff supportive upper garment of female dress.

BODGER Skilled craftsman who made wooden chair legs and spars using a lathe set up in home-made workshops in deep woodlands. His work was often produced for chair factories.

BODY IRONER A laundry worker engaged in ironing the starched parts of shirts on a special ironing machine.

BOILER PLATER Iron worker employed in manufacture of rolled iron plate used for making steam boilers etc.

BOKELER A maker of buckles.

BOLL One who managed power looms.

BOLSTER/BOWLSTER see Bowler.

BOLTER 15c NFK. A sifter of meal.

BONDAGER Female farm worker, who lived in and was often the servant of the Hind (q.v.). Worked mainly out of doors in the fields.

BONE BUTTON TURNER Skilled worker who shaped and trimmed buttons on a lathe.

BONE CLEANER Servant.

BONE LACE MAKER Pillow lace maker. The bobbins on which the lace was made were made of bone.

BONE MOULD TURNER Maker of moulds from bone, probably for button makers.

BONE PICKER A collector of rags and bones.

BONESETTER One with special skills in manipulating injured or broken limbs.

BOOK-KEEPER One who kept accounts for merchants, tradesmen, manufacturers etc.

BOOKSMAN A Clerk or Secretary.

BOONMASTER An officer of the parish appointed as Surveyor of Highways under an Act of 1555. He was obliged to carry out a survey three times a year and organise labour to repair the roads. Any landowners who did not provide the statute labour would be liable for a fine which the Boonmaster was responsible for collecting.

BOOTBINDER In shoemaking factory worker who operated machine which bound the leather edges on boots & shoes.

BOOTCATCHER Inn Servant who pulled off guests boots.

BOOT CLOSER Machinist in shoe factory who fitted together the pre-cut parts of the upper boot. Until the introduction of the Singer Sewing Machine in mid 19c. this had been done by hand by outworkers. Further mechanisation led to building of shoe factories in 1860's.

BOOTLACE DOZENER Made up finished laces into bundles of a dozen pairs.

BORLER A clothier. see Bureler.

BORSHOLDER A superior Constable.

BOSOM IRONER see Body Ironer.

BOTTILER/ BOTTLER Made leather bottles or cases for holding liquids or solids.

BOTTLE BOY An apothecary's assistant.

BOTTOM CUTTER Mine or quarry worker who cut stone away from floor of underground roads to increase headroom.

BOTTOM KNOCKER Young boy who assisted saggar maker (q.v.) in pottery mills.

BOTTOM MAKER see Saggar Maker. Pottery worker who moulded bottoms for saggars.

BOTTOM PAINTER Applied waxed ink or paint to soles, edges, and heels of boots, also known as an Inker.

BOTTOMER A pit worker, one who took the excavated material to the bottom of the shaft.

BOTTOM SHOOTER See Bottom Knocker.

BOULTERER Cod fisherman, also known as a Longliner.

BOWDLER 14c. SAL. A worker in iron ore. See Puddler

BOWKER 1. Butcher, 14c Preston LAN, 2. Bleacher of fibres, yarns etc. 18c Warrington LAN.

BOWL CAKE MAKER Maker of compressed cakes of cotton for use in buffing machinery.

BOWLER 1. A worker who shaped the bowl of a metal spoon made separately from the handle (14c. NFK), 2. Maker of wooden bowls and dishes, a common rural craft.

BOWLMAN/WOMAN A stoneware merchant, a seller of crockery,

BOWLMINDER YKS. Woollen mill worker who looked after the large iron pans in which wool was washed before carding.

BOWYER 1. Maker of and dealer in bows, 2. An archer.

BOZZLER A parish constable or sheriff's officer.

BRAIDER Net maker. With the 17c. expansion of the Newfoundland cod industry, demand for nets and netting was so great that all children in villages around Bridport were taught the craft from an early age (DOR).

BRAILLER 13c. LND. Maker of girdles.

BRASIATOR A brewer.

BRASS CUTTER Maker of copperplate engravings.

BRASS FOUNDER One who founds or casts brass goods.

BRAYER One who brayed or pounded a mortar.

BRAZIER Worker in brass.

BREACH MAKER Worker in gun-making trade.

BREAKMAN see Brickman. 15c. Warrington LAN.

BREWSTER Brewer, originally applied to female occupation.

BRICK BURNER One who attended to a kiln. Brickmaker.

BRICKEL-LAD Lad in brickyard, employed in minor labouring work.

BRICKMAN Bricklayer.

BRIDGEMAN/BRIDGER One who collected tolls at bridges.

BRIGHT WORKER Sorter of sewing needles, removes defective ones.

BRILLIANDEER Diamond polisher.

BROAD COOPER Employed by a brewer to negotiate with publicans.

BROGGER 15c. York. A wool merchant or broker.

BROOM-SQUIRE Maker of besoms or birch brooms, utilising local raw materials in woodland areas.

BROOM DASHER 19c. KEN. A dealer in faggots, brooms etc.

BROTHERER 16c. CHS dial. See Browderer.

BROWDERER 16c. NFK dial. An Embroiderer.

BROW GIRL Female surface worker at a coal pit.

BROWNSMITH Worker in copper.

BUCKLER Buckle maker.

BUCKLE BEGGAR A Fleet Prison "clergyman", one who celebrated irregular marriages.

BUCKLE MAKER A maker of buckles and shields.

BUCKLE TONGUE MAKER Maker of the sharp points which go through the holes in a belt.

BUCKLESMITH see Buckler.

BUCKWASHER Laundress, see Backwasher.

BUDDLE BOY Young worker in tin or lead mine responsible for the vats or buddles used for washing the ore.

BUG DESTROYER Pest controller.

BULLART/BULLWARD A keeper of bulls.

BUMMAREE 18c LND Billingsgate. A speculative buyer at fish market trading between wholesalers and retailers, a middleman.

BUNTER 16c. LND. A Rag & Bone dealer. Also known as a Caffler.

BURELER Maker of borel, a coarse brown woollen cloth, generally worn by the poorer members of medieaval society. (borel-folk)

BURLER A dresser of finished cloth, who used a special knife to remove knots left in after weaving.

BURLEY MAN An officer appointed to enforce byelaws, a constable's assistant.

BUSKER Sewing machinist who made corsets and lingerie.

BUSTLE Skilled furnaceman in metal mill.

BURRGRAILER A comb maker who rounded off the teeth with a grele or file by hand.

BUTNER A Button maker.

BUTTER CARVER A Butter Printer who printed devices in butter.

BUTTOCKER A Miner who cut coal from angles with a pick.

BUTTON BURNISHER A button polisher.

BUTTY One who negotiated contract work in coal mines, then hired labour to carry it out, middleman. Also known as Chartmaster.

BYEMAN/BYEWORKER General term for underground maintenance worker not employed at coal face.

BYREMAN Herdsman of cattle, goats etc.

CABIN BOY 1.Attended cabins on board ship, 2. Attended workmens cabin in quarries, building sites, etc. Also Kettle or Tool Boy.

CABBIE/CABMAN From mid 18c. Driver of a small single passenger vehicle called a coffin cab (due to the shape of its roof). A later version, the London cab, appeared in 1823 when all Cabbies and Cads (q.v.) were licensed by the authorities.

CAD Man employed to look after and water horses at a coach stand. Also known as a Waterman. Many cads became conductors on the early 19c buses and the term was transferred with them. Bus crews were also licensed.

CADDY BUTCHER One who sold horse meat.

CADGER 1. Carrier, especially one who collected dairy produce from farms to sell in towns, 2. Street seller, beggar.

CAFENDER A Carpenter.

CAFFLER see Bunter.

CAINER 18c. Maker of walking sticks.

CAIRD NBL. A tinker.

CALCINER 16c. NFK. One who burned bones and other substances to produce powdered lime.

CALENDER One who lists documents.

CALENDERER/CALENDERMAN Cloth presser and finisher. Operated a machine with two rollers, i.e. a calender.

CAMISTER 19c. A minister of the cloth (from camis, a light loose robe).

CANDLER Made & sold candles.

CAN-DODGER Textile worker who operated machine to separate fibres prior to spinning.

CANDY MAN 19c.DUR A bailiff or process server.

CANTER A vagrant.

CANVASER A manufacturer of canvas.

CAPPER A maker of caps.

CAPTAIN Chief officer, commander of a company, troop or ship, an overseer.

CARDER Textile worker. Operated implement or machine which combed cotton or wool prior to spinning. A worker who raised the nap on finished cloth.

CARDMAKER 1. Maker of carding implement used for combing wool, flax etc. Originally hand held. (from Fr. 'carde'-teasel head) 2. Printer of playing cards.

CARD NAILER/NAILOR 19c. Mill worker who maintained carding machine cylinders in cotton mill. Originally, children were employed to set metal carding teeth in leather for machines.

CARDROOMER Worker in carding room of mill.

CARMAN/CHARMAN 19c. Driver of large vehicle used for public transport, excursions or furniture removal. One who hired out or drove vehicles, a general carrier of goods. (All city carmen were licensed)

CARTER Waggoner (q.v.) Stable headman.

CASHMARIE Fish pedlar who took salt water fish from coast to inland markets.

CATCH-HAND (LIN) Casual worker employed on low grade agricultural work.

CATAGMAN A cottager.

CATCHPOLE A sheriffs officer, a bailiff.

CAULKER One skilled at caulking seams of boats.

CEMMER see Comber. 17c NFK dial.

CHAIN-BEAMER Textile worker who prepared the warp threads for the weaver's loom.

CHALONER Maker of blankets or coverlets (from original place of manufacture, Chalon-sur-Marne.)

CHAMBERER Chamber maid.

CHAMBERLIN Attendant at an inn.

CHAMBERMAN Cold storage worker.

CHAMBER MASTER Boot and shoemaker working in own house, executing contracts for shops, or selling direct.

CHAFF-CUTTER Cutter of chaff (straw) used for stuffing pillows, cushions etc.

CHAISE MAKER Maker of light weight carts made of wicker work.

CHANDLER Dealer in maritime goods etc. Orig. a candle maker, seller. See Candler.

CHANTY MAN A sailor who led singing of work songs on sailing ships, and ensured that sailors worked in unison. Different chants were used to vary the pace needed for each task. Songs became known as shanties.

CHAPELER A hatter.

CHAPMAN Hawker or pedlar. Orig. a buyer or seller. In Middle Ages a travelling merchant, later term used by Londoners for any kind of dealer outside London. In 17-18c. applied to settled shopkeepers in country towns. Petty Chapman was term usually reserved for a pedlar.

CHARTMASTER see Butty.

CHASER An engraver of metals.

CHEESE FACTOR Cheese wholesaler.

CHILDBED-LINEN WAREHOUSE KEEPER 19c/20c various cities & towns. Manager of establishment which hired out bales of bed linen at time of childbirth. Usually paid for by instalments .

CHINGLOR see Shingler.

CHURCH-MASTER Church warden.

CHURCH-REEVE see Church master.

CINDER-WENCH Woman who collected cinders from gas-works to re-sell door to door in poor areas.

CLAPMAN see Bellman, Town Crier.

CLASSMAN 19c SFK term. Unemployed labourer.

CLAVIGER A servant.

CLAY CARRIER Coal pit worker who assisted the Shot Firer (q.v.) with blasting. Clay was used in charge holes.

CLAYMAN/CLEYMAN 1. One who worked in a clay pit, 2. Worker who weatherproofed buildings by covering wattle with clay.

CLICKER 1. In shoemaking, one who cut out the pieces of leather. 2. In printing trade, chargehand who prepared material ready for printing. 3. In textile industry, one who made up a garment, a maker-up.

CLIPPER ON/OFF 20c. DBY. Coal face worker who coupled or uncoupled coal tubs from the hauling rope.

CLOG IRONER Nails the irons on to the soles of clogs.

CLOTHIER/CLOTHESMAN/ CLOTHMAN One engaged in cloth trade; A maker of woollen cloth; seller of cloth and mens clothes.

CLOUTER See Clower.

CLOWER 16c. NFK. Maker of nails. (From French clou).

COACHMAN Driver or attendant of coach. 1. Private, 2. Hackney, 3. Mail (from 1784), 4. Stage, late 17c.

COAL A lamplighter in Newcastle (DUR).

COAL-BACKER/PORTER Coal carrier responsible for measuring and filling 2cwt. sacks of coal from ship, barge or quayside, and loading coal-merchants waggons.

COAL-BEARER See Bearer.

COAL BURNER 15c NFK Maker of charcoal (by charring wood).

COAL-DRAWER Pit worker who dragged loaded wagons along the tunnel by means of a girdle and chain. Frequently a child or woman, also known as a hurrier or putter.(q.v.)

COAL-HEAVER Worker on board coal ship in dock who unloaded the cargo. Similar to coal-porter.

COAL HIGGLER Itinerant coal dealer usually with horse and cart.

COALMETER 18c. NFK. Official appointed to superintend the measuring of coals.

COALRUNNER Pit boy who worked on coal tubs underground.

COAL WHIPPER Unloaded coal from ships in large containers using a mechanical device which necessitated jumping up and down 'whipping or jerking' it onto the deck.

COAST SURVEYOR/WAITER Custom House officer superintending the landing and shipping of goods on the coast.

COBBLER A mender of shoes. Originally he was prohibited from using new leather.

COBLEMAN 18c. NFK. Boatman who worked on flat bottomed fishing vessel.

COD PLACER 19c. STS Pottery worker in charge of placing the saggars or fire proof containers into the firing ovens. (From cod-to enclose in a pod.)

COGMAN Dealer in coarse cloth similar to worsted.

COKER Charcoal maker.

COLLAR CURLER Laundry worker who pressed finished collars into curled shape.

COLLAR MAKER 1. Saddler, maker of horse collars, 2. One who made collars for shirts, etc.

COLLIER Orig. Charcoal Dealer. 2. Coal Miner. 3. Dealer in coals. 4. Man who worked on a collier or coal boat.

COLORATOR A dyer.

COLOUR CARRIER See Lurrier.

COLOUR MAN Responsible for mixing colour dyes used in various industries e.g. textiles, paint manufacture. 2. One who worked with a house painter mixing coloured paint.

COLPORTEUR Hawker of books, newspapers etc, especially one employed by a society to travel about distributing religious books and pamphlets.

COLT Apprentice (West Country).

COMBER In weaving, one who prepared yarn fibres ready for spinning. Combing was the last major process to be mechanised but by 1850 hand combing was almost extinct.

COMBMAKER Maker of wool combing implements which produced a long smooth yarn. 2. Maker of combs for dressing hair.

COMMISSIONER OF STAMP DUTIES Tax official.

CONDER/CONNER 1. Crewman who gave directions to the steersman for guiding a ship. 2. One who signalled, from coastal high ground, to fishing boats, the movement of shoals of fish.

CONFINED MAN Farm Labourer employed on yearly or half yearly agreements.

COOPER Maker and repairer of wooden vessels, e.g. casks & barrels.

COPEMAN A dealer. In 18c. came to mean receiver of stolen goods.

COPPER WOMAN Laundry worker in charge of copper boiler, putting in whites for boiling and removing when clean.

COPSTER Spinner.

CORDINER 18-19c. SCT. Local variant of cordwainer. In 1722 the Cordiners of Hawick petitioned the council to be incorporated & separated from shoemakers or 'those who make single soled shoes'.

CORDWAINER/CORVINER Orig. worker in cordwain (Cordovan leather), not necessarily a shoemaker. Despite opposition from cordwainers in 18-19c. the Company of Shoemakers kept the term as a Trade Guild.

CORNCUTTER A Chiropodist.

CORN-METER A corn measurer, market official.

CORRETIER Horse Dealer

CORVER 18c. Made 'corves', type of basket used in coal mining.

CORVISER/CORVISOR 17c. NFK. A high class shoemaker who only used Cordovan leather. see Cordwainer.

COSIER Cobbler.

COSTERMONGER Itinerant seller of apples and other fruit (From costard, a round bulky apple).

COTELER see Cutler.

COTTAGER/COTTAR Occupier of cottage with small piece of land, held by service of labour to principal farm.

COTTON FEEDER Worker in cotton mill who fed cotton into the loom prior to spinning.

COTYLER See Cutler

COUCHER Skilled worker in paper mill responsible for a specific process in paper-making.

COUPER One who barters, deals or buys and sells. Orig. dealer in horses and cattle. Sometimes mis-spelt as cooper.

COUPLE-BEGGAR An itinerant priest who performed marriages irregularly i.e. without banns or licence. Hardwicke's Marriage Act of 1754 legalised such marriages but the officiating minister was declared a felon.

COURTIER Owner or driver of a small horse drawn cart or 'court'.

COURT FACTOR Dealer of courts, small tip-carts used by farmers and various traders to carry root crops, stones, bricks, sand, etc.

COURT ROLLER One responsible for keeping the Rolls of a Law Court.

COURT TOOLMAKER Maker of tools used in manufacture of 'courts'. See Court factor.

COURSER Groom, Stablehand.

COWKEEPER Kept cow(s). A common source of livelihood in cities and towns was a cow kept in the backyard of a house, providing milk which was sold at front door or window, forerunner of the local dairy.

COW LEECH Animal 'doctor', veterinary practitioner.

COZIER Tailor.

CRABBER Textile worker operating machine to flatten and smooth woollen or worsted fabric.

CRACKER-OFF Glass worker responsible for removing surplus glass from glassware.

CRAPPER Slate-maker who worked in quarry all year round. See Digger.

CRATE-MAN STS. An itinerant seller of earthenware .

CRIMP 1. Ensnared people to man ships often employing services of the press gang. 2. Dealer in coals (NFK).

CROCKER Maker of crocks, a potter.

CROFTER 1. Bleacher of textiles, 2. A Smallholder.

CROKER A grower of saffron, crocus used for making colouring.

CROPPER A Shearman.

CROWKEEPER see Bird-Boy.

CRUNNER Coroner.

CRUTCHER Soapmaker, also Pan Man.

CROWNER A coroner.

CURRIER One who dressed and coloured leather after the tanning process, originally linked with cordwainers (q.v.).

CURSITOR Chancery Court clerk who drew up wills.

CUSTOS Warden, keeper, guardian.

CUTLER Maker of knives and other cutting implements. Also sold and repaired knives, etc.

DAITIER Dairyman.

DAMPERMAN Operator of damping machine used in fabric finishing process.

DANTER Female superintendent of winding room in silk mill.

DANTMAN Colliery labourer who loads residue "dant" from colliery washery into removal trucks (LAN).

DARRICKER A casual worker, odd job man.

DAUBER One who built walls with clay or mud; a plasterer.

DAY-MAN A labourer hired by the day.

DAYTALEMAN See Dayman.

DECOYMAN Employed to decoy wild fowl in shoots.

DECRETIST One versed in decretals, decrees, esp.of the Pope.

DEEMER/DEEMSTER/DEMPSTER A Judge.

DELVER Man who dug ditches.

DEPARTER A refiner of metals.

DEVIL Printers errand boy.

DEVILLER Textile worker who operated a rag-tearing machine called a 'devil'.

DEXTER A Dyer.

DEY Originally a female servant who had charge of the dairy and all things pertaining to it, sometimes applied to a male servant.

DEY-WIFE A dairywoman.

DIGGER 1. A miner who dug out minerals, a coalface worker. 2. Labourer employed in stone or slate quarry for short periods at a time, very little work being available all year round .

DIKEMAN A hedger or ditcher.

DILKER Worker paid by the day, a Dataler (LAN).

DIPPER 1. Pottery worker responsible for glazing process. 2. Tinplate worker responsible for actual tinning process.

DIRECTORY COMPILER Visits business premises and dwelling houses in a prescribed area, compiles lists of names and addresses of occupants according to trades, professions, etc, for an editor, collects information regarding description of town, checks entries for annual re-issue. Solicits adverts.

DIS-HAND Print Worker responsible for replacing type after printing is complete.

DISTRAINING BROKER Carries out distraints for debts on goods, furniture etc, under a bill of sale or order of court, effects entry to prsmises, values and removes goods to cover amount of debt.

DISHER 14c SOM. A maker of bowls or dishes.

DOFFER Textile worker who removed full bobbins and spindles from loom or one who worked on carding machines.

DOG KILLER A person employed by the parish to kill any dogs found running loose during hot weather.

DOG WHIPPER 1. Appointed to deal with dogs disturbing church services, especially when fox tails were nailed to church door as evidence of capture for bounty (common practice from Middle Ages). 2. Mine superintendant responsible for pony drivers working underground.

DOGGER Worker in processing of metal.

DONKEY BOY/MAN 1. Driver of carriage hired by public passengers. 2. Supervisor in charge of boilers in ship's engine room, 3. Driver of winch on shore.

DONKEY MAKER Cabinet maker working in deal, fir, and other soft woods.

DORCAS A seamstress.

DORNIX WEAVER Maker of Dornix, a coarse damask used for curtains, wall hangings, and carpets.

DOUBLER Operator of machines used to compress several fibres of silk, cotton, wool, etc., the process of doubling.

DOWSER A diviner of water or mineral, one who claims the skill to locate underground sources of water or mineral by holding forked hazel twigs above.

DRAGOMAN 1. An Arabic/Turkish interpreter. 2. A guide.

DRAGMAN A fisherman who used a net drawn on the bottom of a river.

DRAGSMAN One who managed a drag, a small type of stage-coach or carriage used for public transport and private use. Drivers were noted for their smart dress hence 'swell dragsman.'

DRASHER Thresher.

DRAWBOY A weavers assistant, particularly in shawl making.

DRAWER 1. Man who raised the coal up the shaft and banked it on the surface. 2. Worker in metal, making wire or tube by pulling or drawing through a die.

DRAYMAN Driver of a dray, a low heavily constructed four-wheeled cart such as used by brewers.

DRESSER 1. Operator of machine which prepared threads in textile industry, 2. One who prepared metal, food, fields, etc. 3. Surgeon's assistant, one who dressed wounds.

DRIBBLE A drudge or servant.

DRIPPING-MAN A dealer in dripping, fat collected from cooked meats.

DROVER One who drove animals to market, a cattle dealer.

DROWNER Man who tended a water meadow.

DRUM-BATTLEDORE MAKER 1864 LND. Maker of galvanised drums fitted with paddles used in washing machines and other mechanical agitators. A battledore was a bat-shaped beater.

DRYSALTER see Salter . Dealer in salted or dry meats, pickles, sauces, etc., and certain chemical products, such as gums and dye-stuffs.

DRY SOAP MAKER Soap powder maker.

DUBBER Trimmer or binder of books (YKS).

DUFFER Pedlar of women's clothes.

DUKEY RIDER 1. Railway guard's assistant who coupled and uncoupled train carriages. 2. Railway worker at coalpit either on surface or underground.

DUNG BOY City street road sweeper.

DUNG-FARMER Jakes Farmer. Person who cleaned out privies, cess pits etc.

DUSTYFAT Pedlar.

DUSTYPOLL Miller (Nickname)

EARTH STOPPER 19c. CUL. One who stopped up the entrance to a foxes earth prior to a hunt.

EGGLER Egg dealer, poulterer.

ELEPHANTS TEETH DEALER See Ivory Workers.

ELLERMAN/ELLIMAN Seller of oil used for lamps.

ENGINEER 1. Designer of bridges, roads etc, 2. Soldier, 3. Operator of an 'engine' in the sense of a machine in textile industry, or of any steam driven machine.

ENGINE TENTER see Tenterer.

ENGRAVER Cutter or carver of designs in metal, stone, wood etc. In textile industry one who engraved plates for printing patterns on fabrics.

ENGROSSER One who purchased large quantities of a commodity to sell at an enhanced price.

EWE-HERD 14c. YKS. A shepherd.

EYER In needlemaking one who made the eyes in the needles. Also referred to as a Holer.

FACTOR 1. An agent employed by merchants to transact business of buying and selling, 2. A Scottish term for the steward of an estate responsible fo collection of land rents.

FAGETTER One who made up faggots into bundles, seller of firewood.

FAKER 19 & 20c. Photographic assistant who added colour to photographs by hand before colour film was available.

FALL MAKER Specialises in making piano lids.

FANCY-PEARL WORKER Worked in 'mother-of-pearl' making buttons or fancy goods.

FANG MANAGER Pit foreman responsible for examining the shafts daily, travelling down on top of the pit cage.

FANWRIGHT 16c. NFK. Maker and repairer of fans or winnowing baskets.

FARANDMAN A stranger or traveller, especially a travelling merchant.

FARMAN Hawker, pedlar.

FARRIER 1. Shoeing smith, 2. Horse doctor, 3. Non-commissioned officer responsible for the shoeing of horses of a cavalry regiment.

FAT BOY/LAD Quarry worker responsible for greasing the axles of wagons, and general odd jobs . Also Wheel boy.

FAW Itinerant tinker, potter etc.

FEAR-NOTHING MAKER 18c. NFK. Weaver of special kind of thick woollen cloth known as FEAR-NOUGHT, used for protective clothing and lining portholes, walls, and doors of powder magazines on board ships.

FEATHER-BEATER Cleanser of feathers. Also F. Driver.

FEATHER-DRESSER One who cleaned and prepared feathers for sale.

FEATHERMAN A dealer in feathers and plumes.

FEATHER-WIFE Woman who prepared feathers for use.

FEEDER Servant.

FELLER 1. Textile worker who laid or felled seams in material. 2. Tree or wood cutter.

FELLMONGER Dealer in hides and skins esp. sheep.

FELTER See Beaver. One who made or worked with felt.

FELTMAKER Generally referred to a worker in the hatting industry.

FENT SORTER Dealer of scraps from a textile warehouse.

FERMERERE Officer in charge of the infirmary.

FERONER Ironmonger.

FERRER Farrier.

FERRETER Dealer in or manufacturer of ferret, i.e. silk tape.

FESTITIAN 15c. NFK Mis-spelling for physician.

FETTLER 1. Cleaned the machinery in woollen mills, removing accumulated fibres, grease, etc. 2. In CHS. fettlers sharpened the fustian cutters knives. 3. Needle-maker who filed the needle to a point.

FEWSTER 14c. YKS. Maker of saddletrees.

FEWTERER 13c. SSK Keeper of hounds, for hunting or coursing.

FEYDUR BEATER Feather Beater 19c. DBY.

FIELD MASTER see Hayward.

FILLER 1. One who filled bobbins in mills.

FINE DRAWER 18c. LND. Employed in tailoring to repair tears in the cloth. 'Invisible mending'.

FINER Worker in a wrought iron finery.

FINISHER Operated machine giving final touches to a manufactured article in various trades. e.g. Cloth finisher. Also craftsman who hand finished an article as in bookbinding.

FIRST HAND Silk weaver who had his own loom. An outworker.

FISCERE A fisherman. (A/S)

FITTER Orig. applied to a joiner. In 19c. common term for one who assembled several portions of machinery together.

FLASHER A specialist process worker in the glass industry.

FLAT HAND Maker of flat brushes e.g. whitewash brushes.

FLATMAN Navigated a flat, a broad flat bottomed boat used for transport esp.in shallow waters. Common in CHS salt trade.

FLAXDRESSER Prepared flax prior to spinning.

FLESHER/FLESHEWER A butcher, a slaughterman.

FLESHMONGER See Flesher.

FLETCHER Arrowsmith. (from Fr. fleche)

FLOATER Vagrant.

FLOATMAN see Flatman.

FLOCK MERCHANT Dealer in flocks, a waste product from the manufacture of shoddy.(wool industry)

FLOWER 13c. DEV. Archer (Flo = arrow)

FLUSHERMAN One who cleaned out water mains.

FLUTTERGRUB A field labourer.

FLY COACHMAN See Jobmaster. 19c. LND. Driver of one horse carriage hired by the day.

FLYING STATIONER 18c. A street broadsheet seller.

FLYMAN 19c. LND. 1. Driver of a light vehicle hired out for carriage of passengers. 2. 20c. Theatre stage hand.

FOAL Young boy employed in mine to help pull coal tubs.

FODDERER See Fogger 3.

FOGGER 1. Petty chapman carrying wares from village to village, 2. Middleman in nail & chain trade. 3. Agricultural worker responsible for feeding the animals. 4. Low class lawyer (Pettifogger).

FOISTER/FOISTERER 15c. NFK. Joiner.

FOOT-BOY/MAN A servant or attendant in livery. See Tiger.

FOOT-POST A letter carrier or messenger who travelled on foot.

FOOT STRAIGHTENER In watchmaking, one who assembled watch and clock dials.

FOOTER Stocking machinist who made the foot.

FORGEMAN 1. Blacksmith or assistant. 2. Coachsmith (18c. DBY).

FORGER 16c. NFK. Blacksmith, worker at a forge.

FORKNER 17c. SFK. Falconer. (misspelling)

FORWARDER Craftsman in bookbinding trade who did all the structural work before it was decorated.

FOSSETMAKER One who made faucets for ale-casks etc..

FOSSIL DIGGER Labourer who dug out copralites, used as artificial manure (CAM).

FOSTER A Forester.

FOURBOUR Furbisher, a metal polisher.

FOWER 16c. NFK. Street cleaner, sweeper.

FOWLER A wildfowler, an East Anglian fisherman who also hunted wildfowl by boat on the broads.

FRAME SPINNER Worker on a loom.

FRAMEWORK KNITTER Operator of machine which made hosiery. Originally a hand loom was used.

FRESHWATER MAN Sailed boat on fresh water only or in the coastal trade.

FRESER Maker of frieze, a rough plaster.

FRINGEMAKER One who made fringes, ornamental borders of cloth.

FRITTER Attendant of equipment which subjects materials or products to heat treatment.

FROBISHER see Furbisher.

FRUITESTERE Female fruit seller.

FULKER A pawnbroker.

FULLER See also Tucker & Walker. Term found mainly in S & E. England. Originally one who used fullers earth to thicken and cleanse cloth , treading it under water.

FURBISHER 15c. NFK. Remover of rust, a polisher of metal e.g. armour.

FURNER MASTER One who has charge of an oven; a baker.

FURRIER Dealer and dresser of furs.

FUSTERER Maker of pack saddles.

FUSTIAN WEAVER Maker of corduroy.

FUYSTER See Foister.

GABERLITIE A ballad singer.

GADGER A gauger or exciseman.

GAFFER 1. Foreman of a gang of workers. 2. An elderly rustic, an old man.

GAFFMAN A bailiff.

GALLOWGLASS A heavily armed Irish foot soldier.

GALVANISER Iron worker who handled process of coating metal with zinc, to inhibit formation of rust.

GAMESTER 1. A gambler. 2. A prostitute (19c. slang)

GANGER Overseer or foreman. 1850 onwards.

GANGEREL Vagabond.

GANGSMAN A Foreman, an overseer.

GANNOKER A Tavern or Innkeeper.

GARTHMAN 1. Yardman or herdsman. 2. One responsible for the upkeep of a garth, a dam built in a river to catch fish.

GARTHYNERE Gardener.

GATE-BOY Child employed to lift a water controlling gate in a tin plate works.(Treforest, S.Wales 1842)

GATER 13c. HUN. A watchman.

GATE-WARD Porter or Gate Keeper.

GATHERER A glassworker who inserted the blow iron into the molten glass ready for the blower q.v.

GATHERERS BOY See Gatherer. One who held a shovel to shield the gatherers face from the heat.

GATWARD 15c. NFK. A goat keeper.

GAUD GATHERER Tax collector (LAN).

GAUGER Customs official who measured the capacity of imported barrels of liquor in order to calculate the customs duty.

GAULTER Digger of marl at chalk quarry.

GAUNT(L)ER 15c. YKS. A glover.

GAVELLER 1. Userer. 2. In the Forest of Dean, an officer of the Crown who granted "gales" or the right to work a mine. 3. In SFK a harvest worker, usually female.

GELDER Castrator of animals, especially horses.

GIMLER Machinist involved in making gimp, a kind of card.

GEOMETER A gauger.

GEOTER Metal caster.

GIRDLER Leather worker who made girdles and belts, chiefly for the Army.

GIRTHOXTER See Girthweaver. 1703 Landkey DEV.

GIRTHWEAVER Web weaver (harness for horses).

GLASS COACHMAN See Jobmaster. 19c. LND. Driver of two horse carriage hired out for the day.

GLASSMAN 1. Glazier. 2. Seller of glassware.

GLAZENER Glazier.

GLE-MAN A minstrel.

GOAT CARRIAGE MAN 19c. LND. Driver of small passenger carriage.

GOFFERER/GOPHERER Laundry worker responsible for smoothing frills of linen using a specially constructed iron.

GOLDIE COOLER Golden syrup cooler, Operative in charge of cooling process during golden syrup making.

GORZEMAN Seller of gorse or broom.

GRAVER 1. Carver or sculptor, engraver of images. 2. Dockside worker who cleaned ship bottoms by burning and tarring.

GREAVE/GRIEVE Bailiff, foreman, sheriff.

GREENSMITH Worker in copper or latten.

GREENWICH BARBER 18c. Retailer of sand collected from the Greenwich pits.

GRINDER 1. One who operated grinding machine. Found in various trades, metal works, knife sharpening, cutlery in general, also glass & toolmaking. 2. Worker who maintained a carding machine (Textile Industry). 3. A private tutor. (slang)

GROOMGRUBBER Officer in the Royal Household responsible for checking barrels and casks in the cellars.

GROOM-PORTER Officer in the Royal Household whose duty was to see the King's lodgings were suitably furnished.

GROUNDSEL & CHICKWEED SELLER A streetseller of common weeds, used to feed pet songbirds.

GUINEA PIG An unattached, or roving parson, whose fee was usually a guinea. (slang)

GULLY MAN Sweeps, cleans , and flushes drains and gullies in and around factories, works, and public buildings.

GUMMER 19c. DBY. One who improved old saws by deepening the cuts.

GYP 18c.CAM, A college servant, especially one attending under-graduates.

HABERDASHER 1. Dealer in small articles e.g. ribbons, needles, pins. 2. Dealer in hats, shirts, ties, collars. 3. Schoolmaster.

HACKER 1. Wood cutter, one who used hoe, axe, or other cutting tools.

HACKLER Worker in linen industry. One who separated the coarse part of flax or hemp with a hackle, an instrument with teeth.

HACKMAN See Hackler. 19c. DBY.

HAFT CUTTER Handle cutter, sometimes specifically named according to the material worked in, e.g. Bone, Ivory.

HAIRMAN See Hairweaver.

HAIR SEATING & CURLED-HAIR MERCHANT Dealer in horse-hair stuffing used in upholstery.

HAIRWEAVER 16c. NFK. Weaver of cloth composed wholly or partly of horsehair.

HALBERT CARRIER A soldier or halberdier, armed with a halberd, a combination spear and battleaxe. A ceremonial officer.

HAMMERMAN A hammerer, a smith.

HAND A doer or workman in any business or work.

HANDSELLER A street vendor.

HAND(Y)WOMAN Local woman called in to help at births and deaths. ("one at hand when coming in and going out")

HANGLER The upper servant on a farm.

HARBEGIER see Harbinger.

HARBINGER Person who had a duty to provide lodgings for their King or Master.

HARLOT 1. 13c. Vagabond, begger, rogue. 2. 14c. A male servant, attendant or menial. 3. 15c. Loose woman.

HARPER 15c. Nfk. Performer on the harp.

HATTER Maker of or dealer in hats.

HAWKER 1. Street seller who cried his wares in a town. 2. Often applied to country pedlars as a term of abuse. 3. Itinerant dealer who carried his wares on his back.

HAYMONGER Dealer in hay.

HAYWARD 1. Inspector of hedges and fences of parish who also impounded stray beasts. 2. Man who tended field set aside to produce hay.

HEADWOMAN A handywoman (q.v.).

HEALD KNITTER An operator of a machine which produced a jersey type of fabric. as opposed to woven fabric. (Textile Industry)

HEALER/HELLIER A slater or tiler.

HECK MAKER Maker of a part of a spinning machine by which the yarn is guided to the reels.

HECKLER See Hackler.

HEDGE LOOKER see Hayward. Supervised good repair of fence and enclosures.also Hedge Tacker (DEV).

HEELMAKER One who made shoe heels.

HELPER-UP Young boy employed in Durham pits to help other workers.

HELLIER/HILLIER Slater or tiler of roofs.

HEMP HECKLER A flax dresser. See Hackler.

HENCHMAN/HENSMAN 16c. LND. A horseman or groom.

HERDESS Shepherdess.

HEUSTER/HEWSTER a dyer.

HEWER Miner who cut coal, stone, etc., a face worker in a mine.

HIGGLER One who haggles or bargains. An itinerant dealer, similar to a cadger.

HILLIER See Hellier.

HIND Farm labourer, household or domestic. servant. In SCT a skilled farm labourer.

HINXMAN See Henchman.

HITCHER Man in charge of cage operations at the bottom of a pit shaft.

HOASTMAN Dealer in sea coal (Newcastle)

HOBBLER Man employed to tow vessels by rope, on land.

HOBELER Light horseman, formerly, certain tenants who were bound to maintain a hobby or pony for use in case of invasion.

HOBLER Sentinels who kept watch at beacons and ran to communicate news.(IoW)

HOCUS-POCUS MAN Street ice cream seller.

HOD A bricklayers labourer.

HOGGARD 17c. A pig drover.

HOLLOWARE WORKER 1. Pottery worker who made ornaments, teapots, etc. as opposed to flatware such as plates, dishes. 2. One involved in the production of tin trunks, chests, boxes,etc. or the painting and graining of them.

HOOKER 1. 16c. Reaper. 2. 19c. Worker in textile industry who operated a machine which laid fabric. flat in uniform folds of any required length.

HOOKER-ON Collier who worked from the cage pushing tubs into the workings.

HOOPER Maker of hoops for barrels or casks.

HORNER Worker in horn making spoons, combs, or musical horns.

HORN OPENER Cuts sections of horn, and flattens it ready for comb making.

HORSE-CAPPER A dealer in worthless horses.

HORSE-COURSER Horse dealer.

HORSE-HAIR CURLER Dressed horse hair which was used extensively in the upholstery trade.

HORSE LEECH Horse-doctor, or Farrier. See Cowleech.

HORSE MARINE Man-handled barges on canals when horses could not be used.

HORSER Worker engaged in cleaning and processing horse hair.

HORSE SINGER Singes horse's coats after clipping to remove loose hairs.Trims horse's coats, manes and tails by hand, usually self employed.

HORSE STOVER Person officially appointed to fumigate a house when an infectious disease had occurred within, or when it was infested with cockroaches, fleas, bugs etc.

HOSIER Retailer of stockings, socks, gloves, nightcaps etc.

HOSTELLER An Innkeeper.

HOSTLER See Ostler. Took care of horses at an Inn.

HOTPRESSER Worker in Paper or Textile industry. Product was pressed between glazed boards and hot metal plates to obtain a smooth and shiny surface.

HOUSE-JEW (19c. LON). A tailor. A ship's tailor took care of the sewing or "jewing" on board, being known as the Jew (naut.)

HOYMAN 19c. LND. One who engaged in the carriage of goods and passengers by water (Hoy = small coastal vessel or sloop).

HUCKSTER 1. Street seller of ale, often a woman. 2. Retailer of small wares in shop or booth.

HUISSHER An usher. A door attendant.

HURDLEMAN/HURDLER A hedgemaker, of wattled framework fencing, a southern counties trade.

HURRIERS 19c. LAN. In coal mining, term applied to the girls aged 5-18 years who were employed as coal-drawers (q.v.).

HUSBANDMAN A tenant farmer.

HUSH SHOP KEEPER 19c. LAN. Brewed and sold beer without a licence (usually as a side line).

IM(P)NER A gardener. (Imp-shoot, cutting of a plant)

INGROSSER see ENGROSSER (CON)

INKLE-WEAVER Maker of coarse narrow tape used for shoe ties,apron strings etc.Sometimes called Beggar's Inkle as it was often made and sold by itinerant beggars.

INNER-GIRL Housemaid in a farm house,kitchen maid. (LIN).

INSIDE SERVANT Servant who lodged with the family.

INTAKER Receiver of stolen goods.

INTERLOPER (NFK) Person with no regular employment.

INWORKER Indoor domestic. servant

IRON FOUNDER One who founds or casts iron.

IRON INDUSTRY Workers included the following : Brazier, Broker, Caster, Founder, Galvaniser, Moulder, Monger, Shearer, Platemaker, Worker.

IRON MONGER Dealer in hardware made of iron. Also known as a Feroner.

IRON SMITH Worker in iron, a Blacksmith.

IVORY NUT CUTTER Cut and fashioned vegetable ivory into required sizes and shapes. The ivory nut or seedpod of the Carozo palm tree was imported from South America as an ivory substitute when natural ivory became expensive.

IVORY WORKERS Included makers of combs, boxes, billiard balls, buttons, and keys for pianofortes.

JACK 1. A young workman. 2. A police officer or detective in plain clothes.

JACK FRAME TENTER Cotton industry worker who operated a jack-frame, used for giving a twist to the thread.

JACK-ABOUT Person not engaged in any particular profession, a jack-of-all-trades.

JACK-SMITH Maker of lifting machinery and contrivances.

JAGGER 1. 14c. YKS. Carrier, carter, pedlar or hawker of fish. 2. 19c. DBY. A young boy in charge of 'jags' or train of trucks in coal mine . 3. Man in charge of pack horse carrying iron ore to be smelted. 4. From 1899 a uniformed messenger boy employed by a London business firm.

JAKES-FARMER One who emptied cesspools.

JAPANNER A varnisher who used lacquering process invented in Japan. Closely allied to Papier-Mache trade.

JERQUER Custom house officer who searched ships.

JERSEY COMBER Worker in woollen manufacture. Jersey = wool which has been combed but not spun into yarn.

JEWS-POKER Person employed to light the fires in Jewish houses on their Sabbath.

JIGGER A constable. (HAN)

JIGGERER Pottery worker who used a jig to mould the clay into flat or holloware goods. Also Jollier.

JIGGERMAN Operator of machine for dying textiles.

JIM CROW A Street Actor.

JIPPER An ink boy, assisted at wood pulp mill.

JOB COACHMAN see Jobmaster. 19c. LND. Driver of coach hired out for long periods to nobility or gentry.

JOBBER 1. Dealer in cattle or livestock 2. Trading middleman who bought the dairy produce of farmers.

JOBLING GARDENER One employed on a casual basis. Also Jobbing.

JOBMASTER Supplied carriages, horses and drivers for hire.

JOCK A Horse Dealer

JOINER A Carpenter. Originally the two trades were distinct, a joiner did light work such as doors and windows, while a carpenter framed the heavy timbers of a house for floors and roofs.

JOLLIER Pottery worker, see Jiggerer.

JOSS Foreman or Overlooker, a Master Employer.

JOTTERY MAN General servant.

JOURNEYMAN Had served an apprenticeship and was no longer bound to serve a master.

JOWDER Hawker, pedlar. (SOM)

JOWSTER Itinerant seller of fish. (CON)

JUSTMAN-HOLDER Freeholder. (DEV)

KAITE A dresser of wool.

KEDGER A Fisherman.

KEEKER DUR. Colliery official who checked quantity and quality of coal output. Also a Weighman.

KEEL BULLY Mate on board a keel.

KEEL DEETER/DIGHTER A Keel cleaner, often a daughter or wife of a Keelman.

KEELER/KEELMAN (Tyneside) A bargeman. From keel, a flat bottomed boat.

KEMPSTER 14c. YKS A woolcomber.

KERNE An Irish foot soldier of the lowest rank.

KERNER Trimmer of typeface, removing surplus metal from castings.

KIDDIER 1. Skinner. 2. Dealer in young goats.

KIERER/KIERMAN Bleacher of yarns, etc. in textile industry.

KILNER A limeburner, in charge of a kiln.

KIRVER Miner who prepared coal seam for hewing, a picksman.

KISSER 14c. LND. Made cuishes & high armour.

KNACKER Dealer in old horses, dead animals. Sometimes Harness maker, saddler.

KNITSTER A female knitter. (DEV)

KNAPPERS Dressed and shaped flints into required shape and size. Major use was flint locks in weapons for British Army.

KNELLER/KNULLER 19c. Chimney sweep who solicited custom by knocking on doors.

KNOCKER-UP Man paid to wake up northern mill & factory workers on early shifts, going from house to house using a long pole to knock on bedroom windows.

KNOLLER A toller of bells.

KOLLERGANGER Machinist in paper works responsible for preparing wood-pulp for paper making. Also Potcherman.

LACE -DRAWER Child employed in lace work, drawing out threads.

LACEMAN Dealer in lace, who collected it from the makers, usually only those who had bought his thread, and sold it in the lace markets.

LACE-MASTER/MISTRESS Person who employed workers in factories or in their homes for the production of lace.

LACE-RUNNER Young worker who embroidered patterns on lace.

LAGRAETMAN A local constable (Law-Rightman).

LAGGER A sailor.

LAIR MAN Responsible for cattle pens at wharves, where cattle are kept overnight.

LANDSMAN Seaman on first voyage.

LANDWAITER Customs officer whose duty was to wait or attend on landed goods.

LATH RENDER(ER) Applied the first coat of plaster onto laths on walls and ceiling. A plasterers assistant.

LATTENER Skilled metal worker who made or worked in latten, a mixed metal resembling brass.

LAUNDER/ESS Washerwoman, one who washed linen.

LAVENDER Washerwoman, from French 'laver' to wash.

LAYER Worker in paper mill responsible for a particular stage in paper making process.

LEACHMAN Surgeon.

LEAPER/LIPPER Basket maker.

LEAVELOOKER Examined food on sale at market.

LEGGER 1. Canal boatman. Barges had to be 'legged' through under-ground tunnels by the men lying flat on deck and 'walking' along the roof or sides, thus propelling the boat along by leg power not horse power. Also Horse Marine. 2. Stocking machinist making the upper and longest part of the stocking.

LEIGHTONWARD A gardener (leighton = a garden).

LETTER CARRIER 18c. Forerunner of local postman. The Post Office appointed a large number of letter carriers in 1722 to make house to house deliveries within a town.

LEYARE Stonemason.

LIGHTERMAN Boatman who worked on a lighter, a large open flat bottomed boat used in loading and unloading ships.

LIMB-TRIMMER Tailor.

LINER/LYNER A flax dresser.

LINKBOY/MAN 1. One who carried a link or torch to guide people through city streets at night for a small fee. Had to be licensed to trade early 19c. 2. Term sometimes applied to a general manservant late 19c.

LISTER/(LITSTER) Dyer of cloth.

LITTERMAN A groom (of horses)

LOADMAN/LODEMAN Carter, carrier.

LODESMAN Ships pilot, guide.

LORESMAN Teacher.

LOBLOLLY BOY 1. An errand boy, 2. Surgeon's assistant on board ship (Naut.)

LOG WOOD GRINDER Preparer of a dye made from logwood, used in textile industry.

LONG-LINER see Boulterer.

LONG SONG SELLER A street seller who sold popular songsheets printed on paper about a yard long.

LORIMER/LORINER See Spurrier. 1. Made spits, bridles, and other metal parts for the harness of horses. 2. Maker of small ironware. 3. Worker in wrought iron.

LOTSELLER A street seller.

LUMPER 1. Dock labourer who discharged cargo of timber. Employed by a Master Lumper, not the Dock Company. 2. Fine-grain Saltmaker, from practice of moulding salt into lumps.

LUM SWOOPER SCT. A chimney sweep.

LURRIER/LURRYMAN Worker in textile printing factory responsible for bringing the colours required from the colour shop to the print room. A Colour Carrier.

MACSTAR Poulterer or Egg seller.

MADERER 13c. LIN. Gathered and sold garlic.

MAID Female domestic. servant. Class included Scullery, Kitchen, House, General, Parlour, Nurse, Laundry, Lady's, etc.

MAIL GUARD 18c. Armed guard, frequently an ex-soldier, employed on the mail coach service, inaugurated in 1784. Later Post Office guards were officially appointed.

MAISE MAKER 16c. NFK. One who made measures for weighing herring catch.

MAKER-UP 1. Garment assembler, one who prepared or 'made up' material to customers requirements. 2. Chemist or druggist, 3. Agent for paraffin.

MAKE-UP MAN Man called upon to make up required gang number to work in another part of the docks. (Liverpool)

MALEMAKER A maker of 'Males', or travelling bags. The term was adopted by the Royal Mail from the bags which carried letters.

MALENDER A Farmer.

MALLINGER Official Cryer of the Court or Town Council.

MALER See Malemaker.

MAN-AND-WIFE Term specified when both a male and female servant were required for domestic service in the same household, not necessarily a married couple. The man was employed in a variety of duties, e.g. butler, porter, gardener, and the woman usually did cooking and general domestic duties.

MANCHESTER MAN also Shrewsbury, Sheffield, etc. Late 18c. A wholesale travelling merchant trading between factory and shopkeeper with goods on packhorses. Sometimes independent, sometimes employed by the manufacturer.

MANCIPLE The Officer in charge of purchasing provisions for an Inn of Court, a college etc.

MANGLE KEEPER A woman who offered use of the 'clothes' mangle to others for a fee.

MANTLE FOREWOMAN A highly skilled dressmaker.

MANTUA MAKER Dressmaker. Mantua = a womans loose gown.

MARBLER One who stained paper or other material, veined in imitation of marble.

MARINER One who obtained a living on the sea in whatever rank, equivalent to an Able Seaman.

MARK-BOY A lad employed by gamblers to mark scores.

MARSHALL Horse doctor or shoesmith.

MARSHMAN 16c. to late 19c. Employed by various landowners to look after marshlands and tend the animals put to graze there for the season. Also Marsh Looker.

MARTIALIST soldier.

MASH MAKER 14c. LND. Maker of the vats or mashels used in the brewing trade for mixing malt.

MASONER Bricklayer.

MASTER One of 3 grades of skill recognised by the Guilds of Crafts. A skilled workman or one in business on his own.

MASTER LUMPER Contractor of labourers at cheap rate of pay. Generally a publican who only hired and paid workmen inside their public houses.

MASTER MARINER A Sea Captain.

MATHER See Mawer.

MATCHET FORGER Knifemaker. From machete, a heavy axe-like knife used as a tool.

MAWER A mower.

MEALMAN 18c. NFK. Dealer in meal or flour.

MECHANIC 1. Manual labourer, working at a trade. 2.Operator of a machine, (less skilled than an engineer).

MELDER 17c. NFK. A corn miller.

MERCATOR A merchant.

MESSAGER A Mower. (DBY)

METALMAN A worker in metals.

MILESTONE INSPECTOR A vagrant, a "gentleman of the road".

MILLER Corn miller, Cloth miller, Saw miller.

MILLINER 1. Seller of fancy wares and articles of apparel, 2. Maker of ladies hats, bonnets etc.

MILLWRIGHT One designed or set up mills and mill machinery.

MINER A worker in a mine, digging for coal, ironstone, lead, tin, etc.

MOCADO WEAVER Weaver of woollen cloth used for making clothes 16-17c. Sometimes called mock velvet.

MOLITOR A miller.

MONDAYMAN See Cottager. One who worked for landowner on Mondays in lieu of rent.

MONTHLY-NURSE Nurse who attended mother and baby during the month of confinement.

MORNING GIRL Domestic servant employed on a part time basis.

MOULDER RUNNER Pottery moulders assistant, a young boy who ran between master and drying oven carrying full moulds and returning with empty ones.

MUFFIN MAKER Baker who made muffins, round flat cakes of dough, toasted before eating. 2. Pottery worker who made a specific type of plate i.e. a seven inch tea plate known as a muffin.

MUFFIN MAN Itinerant seller of muffins.

MUFFLEMAN Worker in an iron foundry, in charge of a muffle furnace.

MUGGER See Pigman.

MUGSELLER Seller of cups, mugs.

MUMPER Traveller (Romany term for non-Romanies on the road).

MURINGER Official appointed to oversee fortification of walls.

MUSTARDER/MUSTARDMAN Made and dealt in mustard.

NARROW WEAVER Weavers of ribbons, livery lace, tapes etc.

NAUMKEAGER Operator of grinding machine used in finishing parts for footwear.

NAUMKEAGER CAPMAKER Maker of abrasive paper products used in grinding machines.

NAPIER Person in charge of table linen in manor house.

NAVIGATOR 1. A sailor, one who navigated. 2. Labourer digging canals, later the railways. A Navvy.

NAVIGOR see Navigator.

NEATHERD A cowherd.

NECESSARY WOMAN Servant responsible for the emptying and cleaning of chamber pots.

NECKER Worker responsible for feeding cardboard into a box making machine.

NEEDLE POINTER 1. In needlemaking a filer or fettler (q.v.). 2. One engaged in the craft of needlepoint embroidery.

NETTER Net maker, using twine made by a roper.

NIGHT SOILMAN/NIGHTMAN Man employed to empty cesspits and ashpits, work carried out at night.

NIGHTWALKER 17-18c. A watchman or bellman.

NIMGIMMER A surgeon.

NIPPER 19-20c. A lorry boy, a youngster employed by carter or wagoner to assist with collection and delivery of goods.

NOIL BAGGER Collects silk waste fibres removed by dresser in silk works.

NOON TENDER 18c. Liverpool Docks. Customs officer who guarded goods on the quay whilst other officers were at dinner.

NORMALISER Worker in processing metal.

NORICE Nurse (A/S)

NORSEL MAKER Netmaker. One who operated a norselling machine designed to make snoods from twisted yarn.

NOTCHIL Town Cryer.

NOW-NOW Itinerant fiddler frequently mentioned by old writers.

OILMAN Sold oil for lamps.

OLITOR A kitchen gardener. "Olitory" was the kitchen garden.

ON-SETTER Collier who worked at the shaft bottom to ensure correct signalling and cage loading procedures were followed.

OPENER Tinplate worker who separated the plates. Traditionally women carried out this work.

ORNAMENTER-OF-HANDKERCHIEFS Person who examined, counted, folded, and boxed them "in an attractive manner".

ORRA MAN 1. Worker in textile factory who did odd jobs. 2. North of England, a skilled handyman on a farm who stood in for other workers on occasion. Sometimes looked after farm machinery.

ORRERY MAKER One who made a mechanical apparatus which showed the movement of the planets. (Named after the inventor, the 4th Earl of Orrery). The trade is often allied with that of clockmaker.

ORRICE WEAVER Designed lace patterns to be woven with silk thread and silk in silver and gold.

ORSEL/OSSEL MAKER see Norsel maker.

OSIER PEELER Removed bark from willow rods or osiers which were used in basket making. A seasonal occupation which mainly employed women and children. Also known as Withy Peelers.

OSTIARY A monastery door keeper.

OSTLER See Hostler.

OSTREGIER A falconer.

OUT-RIDER Bailiff errant employed by the sheriff to summon persons to the courts.

OUTWORKER Worker who carried on his occupation at home rather than in the factory, e.g. cotton weavers in LAN, woollen weavers in YKS, ribbon makers in Coventry, boot and shoe-makers in NTH, lace makers in NTT.

OVER-HOUSEMAN Small wire drawer.

OVERLOOKER Superintendent or overseer, especially in textile mills. Often an hereditary position.

OVERMAN 16c. DUR. Supervisor in colliery who checked miners work and quality of coal mined.

OWLER One who conveyed contraband goods. Smuggler of sheep or wool out of England.

OYSTER DREDGER Crew member on board an oyster fishing boat .

PACKMAN A pedlar, one who travelled about carrying goods for sale in a pack. See also Higgler and Cadger.

PACK THREAD SPINNER Operator of a machine which produced stout thread or twine.

PAD MAKER 17c. NFK. Maker of small baskets used as measures for fruit etc.

PAINTER 1. Workman who coats or colours surfaces of things (woodwork, ironwork, material) with paint. 2. An artist.

PAINTRESS In the pottery industry the skilled craftswoman who hand painted china.

PALINGMAN A fishmonger.

PALISTER YKS. Park keeper.

PANNIFEX A cloth worker.

PANSMITH Skilled metal worker who made pans.

PANTERER The keeper of the pantry, a butler.

PANTLER see Panterer.

PAPAYA MAN 1823 CON. ? Papua Man, merchant or seaman involved in trade with New Guinea.

PAPERER In Needlemaking Industry, worker who prepared needles for sale by inserting or 'sticking' them in paper or cloth.

PAPERHANGER One who hangs pasted paper to walls, a decorator.

PAPER MAKER See Vatman, Coucher, Layer, Sizer.

PARCELMAKER One of the two officers in the Exchequer appointed to make out the parcels of escheators accounts and deliver them to that Court.

PARDONER Frequenter of Pilgrims Way who sold pardons and indulgences.

PARGETER Skilled plasterer who applied ornamental work to buildings especially on timber-framed houses.

PARITOR Church officer who attended magistrates and justices at court for the purpose of executing their orders.

PARKER Person in charge of a hunting park.

PARLOURMAID Usually employed in private and boarding houses where there were no footmen, waiting on table and having charge of china, silver, and glass.

PASSAGE KEEPER 1824 CON. Person employed to keep passages clean and free from rubbish.

PASTELER/PASTERER Pastry maker.

PASTOREL Shepherd.

PATTEN MAKER Maker of wooden soles specifically designed to wear under ordinary shoes to protect from mud. Clog maker.

PATTEN RING MAKER See Patten Maker. The wooden soles or pattens were mounted on iron rings which raised the feet above mud, and which lessened the wear on the soles.

PAVER/PAVIOUR Man paid by the town to see to upkeep of pavements. A layer of paving stones.

PAVYLER Man who erected temporary moveable buildings such as pavilions, tents, etc.

PAWNBROKER One engaged in the business of lending money upon interest on security of articles of personal property pawned or pledged.

PEARL WORKER General term for one working with mother-of-pearl.

PEBBLE-BOSTER A stone breaker, for road making.

PEDER A small farmer (LIN).

PEDASCULE Schoolmaster.

PEDDAR/PEDLAR A house to house retailer who travelled either on foot or pack horse. Generally bought and sold goods for cash.

PEELER 19c. LND slang. See Bobby.

PEELMAKER Maker of bakers wooden shovels used for placing dough in the oven.

PELTERER 16c. NFK. Skinner of animal pelts.

PERFUMER Sells or makes perfumes, or fumigates.

PERCHEMEAR A parchment maker.

PERUKE/PERIWIG MAKER Wig maker.

PETER MAN 18c. LND. A fisherman.

PETTY CHAPMAN Itinerant dealer in small goods, hawker, pedlar.

PEWTNER Pewterer.

PEW OPENER Hired to open doors of private pews in church.

PHILOSOPHICAL INSTRUMENT MAKER Maker of scientific. instruments.

PICKER In weaving, person who cast the shuttle on a loom.

PICKLER Tinplate worker in charge of cleaning process.

PICKSMAN see Kirver.

PIECE BROKER Retailer of remnants of material.

PIECENER/PIECER A child or young person employed in a spinning mill to piece together any threads which broke.

PIECEMASTER Middleman who acts between employer and employee in giving out piecework to worker.

PIECE WORKER Worker paid according to number of things (or pieces) produced, rather than by hours worked. Outworkers were usually paid by piecework.

PIGMAKER 1. Manufacturer of pig or cast iron. 2. Pottery worker.

PIGMAN See Mugger. 1. A seller of crockery (Pig = common earthen-ware). 2. Farmer who raised pigs or a labourer who looked after them.

PIKELET MAKER Baker who specialised in pikelets, flat cakes made of dough. Depending on the locality these can be of various sizes and shapes, or are known by different names e.g. crumpets, muffins.

PIKEMAN 1.19c. Birmingham, Millers assistant. 2. Man in charge of turnpike. 3. Soldier who carried a pike. 4. (STS) Miner who breaks down coal from cut seams.

PIKER A tramp, one who is always on the road.

PILL-BOX BOTTOMER (19c. DBY). Pottery worker responsible for making bottoms for pill boxes.

PILL-BOX LIDDER Potter who made lids for pill boxes.

PILLOW BEARER 20c. Employed as part of the Official Court Retinue of H.M. Haile Selassie of Ethiopia. The pillow was placed at the feet of the diminutive Emperor to ensure dignity when travelling abroad.

PIN-BOY Weaver's assistant responsible for pinning together broken warp ends in the loom until the weaver was free to mend them .

PINDER Pound keeper. Officer in charge of pinfold.

PINNER Maker of pins.

PINNER-UP 1. A street vendor of broadsides and ballads. 2. A dressmaker's assistant.

PISTOR A baker.

PIT BROW LASS Young female worker at coal pit surface.(LAN)

PITCHER Man who lifted the reaped corn or hay onto the wagon.

PLAICHER See Pleacher. YKS dialect.

PLAIN WORKER Needlewoman who did plain sewing or needlework as distinct from fancy work or embroidery.

PLAISTERER Plasterer.

PLAITER Maker of the straw plaits which were in demand for hats, bonnets, etc. A major cottage industry.

PLANKER In hat making, worker who planks or kneads hat bodies in the process of felting them.

PLASHER See Pleacher. CUL dialect.

PLATCHER See Pleacher. HER dialect.

PLATER See Hooker.

PLAYCHER See Pleacher. WOR dialect.

PLAYDERER 17c. Ulverston LAN. Maker of plaid, a coarse woollen cloth.

PLEACHER Hedge layer, term in general use throughout country. Variants include Plaicher, Plasher, Playcher.

PLOUGH-JOGGER Ploughman.

PLUMASSIER One who made or sold ornamental feathers.

PLUMER Dealer in feathers.

PLUMETTE MAKER One who makes small feather plumes by hand

PLUMBER Originally one who worked in lead, the term came to mean a skilled tradesman who installed and repaired pipes made of all kinds of material for water, gas, drains etc.

POINTER Sharpens objects to a point, needles, pins etc.

POINTMAKER/MAN 16c. Nfk. Maker of points for laces which fastened clothes together, breeches to doublet etc. Those on codpieces were often made of silver, and it was the custom after a wedding for the groom to cut off these points and throw them to the guests before retiring to the bridal bed.

POINTSMAN 19c. Railway worker who changed points to divert trains from one track to another.

POLDAVE WORKER 17c. NFK. One who made poldave, a coarse fabric. or sacking originally woven in Brittany. In 16c. several Bretons were paid to come to England and teach the art of making it to Norfolk weavers.

POLE LATHE TURNER Wood craftsman. See Bodger, Treenmaker.

POLLER/POWLER A barber. (from distinctive pole displayed)

POM-POM MAN One who operates a coal cutting machine.

PONDERATOR Inspector of weights and measures, especially in market towns.

PORTABLE SOUP MAKER Specialist Cook. Dried soup was made into small solid cakes convenient for storage and carriage. Easily reconstituted by the addition of water as and when needed.

PORTER 1. One employed to carry burdens. 2. Person in charge of door, gate etc.

POSSESION MAN Broker's Bailiff.

POST-BOY 1. 18c.Post Office Letter Carrier travelling between towns on horseback. 2. Guard who rode at the back of the Mail coach , often an ex-soldier. 3. Outrider who accompanied stage coach as postillion (q.v.). 4. Glassworker, a tube maker's assistant.

POSTILLION 18c. Employed on long distance stage coaches to change horses at official 'posts' or inns. See Post Boy.

POSTER CUL. A quarryman, a hewer of rock.

POSTMAN The term officially replaced Letter Carrier in 1883 when parcels as well as letters were carried.

POTATO-BADGER Dealer in or seller of potatoes.

POT BOY/MAN Menial worker in a public. house.

POT BURNER In pottery making process worker who placed finished pot in furnace.

POTCHER MAN see Kollerganger.

POTTER CARRIER see Apothecary.

POTTER PRESSER Potter who used a mould to shape the clay.

POTTER THROWER Potter who worked with clay 'thrown' onto a wheel.

POUCH MAKER Maker of leather purses or pouches. The Norman term Purser came to identify a more official position.

POULTER/ER Dealer in poultry and game.

POUNDKEEPER See Pinder.

POYNTER 16c. Maker of laces.

POWDER-MONKEY Shot Firer's assistant (coalmining)

POWER LOOM TUNER Mechanic. who maintained the looms in a textile factory.

POLER Barber, from the red and white pole placed outside the shop. 'Powler' in some dialects.

PRECEPTRESS School mistress.

PRICKER 1. Pattern maker (leather, paper, material,etc) 2. Horseman, one who trained horses.

PRINTER Person who prints in any sense of the word. In textile areas term usually refers to calico printer or printer of patterns on material.

PROP BOBBY DUR Colliery worker responsible for checking on props in mine.

PUD(D)LER 1. One who worked clay, etc. into puddle (paste) see also Pugger. 2. One who lined something with puddle to make it water-tight e.g. canal walls, ponds etc. 3. Worker employed in puddling iron, tending and feeding furnaces.

PUGGER Worker employed in brick fields to make clay paste by the method of treading the clay under bare feet. In some areas where brickmaking was family work it was the job of the children to do the pugging.

PULLBOY Hat blockers assistant, pulled hat over wooden block to set shape, or positioned cloth cap covers over foundation material.

PULLEYMAKER Maker of grooved wheels used in hoisting apparatus.

PULLEY-UP BOY Lad in charge of horse used to pull trams up steep roads. The horse was held on standby at the bottom, harnessed, then released at top of the incline and led down.

PUMPMAKER Maker of pumps and pipes for the raising and lowering of water.

PUNDER See Pinder.

PUNTY STICKER Glassworker, see Gatherer.

PURSER A Paymaster. Originally a Purse or Pouchmaker (q.v.).

PUSHER ON/UP see Shunter.

PUTTER DUR Young boy employed down coalmine , supplying workers with empty tubs and removing full ones. Called Trammers in Yorkshire.

PUTTER-IN Various trades. In 19c. Birmingham applied to child worker in a button factory who fed strip metal into the button stamping presses.

PYROTECHNIST Skilled firework maker in charge of setting up displays, travelling as required.

QUARREL PICKER 17-18c. A glazier. Pun on 'quarrel' a small pane of glass or a tile. (O/Fr.)

QUARRIER Worker in a quarry, a quarryman.

QUENCHER Worker employed in coke-making process to cool the red hot product with water.

QUILLER 1. In Textile Industry operator of machine which wound yarn onto spools. 2. One who quilled material, as in ruffs.

QUILTER/QUILTRESS 1. Sewer who made up padded material using several layers and stitched in specifically designed patterns or lines as for canvas, sailcloth, bed or mattress covers. 2. Maker of cricket ball centres, using worsted thread wrapped around a cork to make the quilt or core of the ball.

QUISTER A Bleacher.

QWYLWRYGHTE Wheelwright.

RACK MAIDEN CON. Girl employed in a tin mine to dress ore.

RADMAN A horseman.

RAFFMAN 1. Collector of rubbish/trash. A dealer in raff-any rubbish which was saleable. 2. Chandler , maker of tallow candles.

RAG CUTTER In agricultural areas woollen rags were used as manure, women being employed to chop them into very small pieces. Rags were also used in the making of paper. The process of rag-cutting was mechanised in 19c. when shoddy mills were set up. See Deviller.

RAG GATHERERS Children or young people employed in woollen mills to clear rags from machinery.

RAG-MAN Itinerant collector and seller of old clothes, rags etc.

RAG-PICKER One who picked over or sorted rags for re-use by a manufacturer. Used extensively in the paper-making industry.

RAKER Man who raked and removed filth from the streets.

RANDER Basker Maker using single osiers rather than plaits.

RANSACKER Worker who sorted and overhauled fishing nets brought into a net warehouse for repair. (East Anglia)

RAPPERMAN Pitshaft worker responsible for giving signals at entrance when miners were taken down.

RASPER Logwood Grinder.

REDSMITH A goldsmith.

REEDER 15c. NFK. Reed layer, thatcher.

REEDMAKER 1. In textile areas, maker of an implement used by tapestry weavers, 2. Maker of pipes used in musical instruments.

REELER Textile worker who operated machine which wound yarn onto a reel or bobbin.

REEVER See Shriever. 13c. LND, 15c. NFK.

RENOVATOR A repairing tailor.

RICK CROWDER Thatcher. Constructs roof coverings for ricks and stacks.

RICKMASTER 18c.SCT. Corruption of "Rittmaster", a Captain of Horse.

RIDDLER Textile industry. A wool stapler.

RIFTERE A reaper. (A/S)

RIPP(I)ER 1. Man who brought fresh water fish into market for sale to the public. 2. Nickname for maker or seller of baskets. 3. Worker in coal mine who broke new ground by tunnelling or "ripping."

ROAD FETTLER (YKS) Underground roadway repairer.

ROCKMAN Stone Quarrier who worked on the rockface placing explosive charges.

ROCKGETTER 18c. CHS. Miner of rocksalt.

ROKSTER 14c. Synonymous with Spinster. Rock was the old distaff.

ROLLER COVERER In Textile Industry, worker who covered rollers for the spinning process.

ROLLEYWAY MAN Attended to the horse road in a mine.

ROLL TURNER 18c. Portsmouth. Prepared carded wool, cotton, intorolls ready for spinning -see Rover.

ROMAN CEMENTER/ PLASTERER & COLOURER 1830 Birmingham Directory. Plasterer skilled in use of Roman cement, for stucco work. (orig. made from Sheppey stone in 1796.)

ROPER Rope or net maker.

ROVER 19c. LAN. Operator of a machine used in cotton spinning, which prepared carded fibre into loose rolls. See Billier.

RUBBISHER/RUBBLER Young boy who sorted 'debris' in a quarry.

RUDDLE-MAN A digger of red chalk known as ruddle, reddle and raddle. Used to mark sheep and redden bricks on old houses.

RUGMAN Seller of rugs.

RUNAFORE BOY Pit lad who ran messages.

RUNNER 19c. LND. A magistrates officer.

RUSH WORKER Harvester or plaiter of rushes, used in production of various articles, baskets, hats, horse-collars, and chairseats. In the Norfolk Broads and Fen districts the whole family could be involved in this cottage industry.

SADDLER Skilled leather worker who made horse collars, harnesses saddles etc.

SADDLE-TREE MAKER Manufacturer of wooden frames used by saddlers.

SAGGAR MAKER Pottery worker who made fireclay containers in which fine stoneware was placed prior to being fired in the oven.

SALESMAN 18c. A shopkeeper who bought ready made goods for sale as opposed to one whose goods were made on the premises, e.g. boots and shoes, furniture. Anyone engaged in the busines of selling merchandise especially wholesale.

SALT BOILER Boiler of salt water (to obtain salt).

SALTER/DRYSALTER Maker of, or dealer in, salt.

SANDCAKE MAKER Foundry worker who made bricks of dried sand used to support castings.

SANDKNOCKER 1. Grinder and seller of sand, commonly used on flagged floors for cleaning purposes. Also, traditionally, sand was scattered in ornamental patterns outside a bride's home at her wedding. (LAN/CHS) 2. Foundry worker who removed or knocked sand from castings.

SAND-RAT Moulder in an iron foundry (LAN) see Sandknocker.

SANDSTONE BRAYER Itinerant seller of powdered sandstone (YKS)

SARCINET WEAVER Silk weaver.

SAUCER 15c. NFK. A salt dealer.

SAWYER Workman whose business is to saw timber, especially in a timber pit or mill.

SAY WEAVER Maker of Say, a fine serge material used for wall hangings/bed/table covers. In 16c. sometimes made from silk.

SCABBLER Quarryman who roughly shaped stone into blocks.

SCAGLIOLA MAKER Maker of imitation marble.

SCALERAKER See Scavenger.

SCAPPLER Stone worker who roughly shaped stone with hammer prior to completion by the Stonemason.

SCARFER Worker in steel foundry who removed defects from metal.

SCAVELMAN KEN. Man employed to scour and clean waterways, and ditches.

SCAVENGER A man employed by parish to clear streets of refuse. A street cleaner.

SCOPPLER Stone-quarry worker.

SCOTCH DRAPER (also Scotchman). 18-19c. House to house retailer who specialised in new type of factory made goods, arranging payment by instalments. Usually on commission for a small firm, occasionally independent. (From Scot-a tax or rate levied in a parish, which was assessed acording to income.)

SCREENER Surface worker at mine who screened out mineral produced. Women and girls were widely employed in this work.

SCRIBBLER 19c. DBY. Textile worker employed in a scribbling mill, where wool was roughly carded prior to spinning etc.

SCRIBER (At docks) worked alongside the Weighter marking unloaded cargo with appropriate weight. Cotton bales were marked in a special code for the brokers who arranged the sale of the cargo inside the warehouse.

SCRIPTURE READER 19c. Worked under the control and direction of parochial clergy. Visited house to house reading scriptures, encouraging church attendances, baptisms, confirmation etc.

SCRIVENER 16c. Clerk specialising in drawing up bonds.

SCUTCHER A worker who beat bundles of flax with a scutching bat, to soften any straw in them.

SEAL-PRESSER 18c. DBY. Glass worker. During process of manufacturing float glass one who sealed the bath against oxygen intake.

SEARCHER See Jerquer. Customs official.

SEEDSMAN Foreman on a farm, responsible for sewing the seed.

SEER An Overlooker. (SOM)

SEGGAR MAN (CUM) see Bottom Cutter.

SELF ACTING MINDER A worker who was in charge of an automatic. spinning mule in textile mill.

SEMI-LORER Maker of leather thongs. (Lore = thong).

SEMPSTRESS Seamstress. Needlewoman whose occupation was plain sewing as distinguished from dressmaking, embroidery etc.

SENESCHAL Senior steward of a medieval lord.

SENSTERE Seamstress

SEWER Upper servant who set and removed dishes at table, tasting and testing them.

SEWER HUNTER One who searched sewers for objects of value, a scavenger.

SEWER-OF-THE-CHAMBER An officer in the Royal or Noble household who came before the Meat and placed it on the table.

SEWER RAT A bricklayer who worked in sewers building and repairing tunnels.

SEWSTER Seamstress.

SHAGREEN CASE MAKER Shagreen = a sort of rough green leather.

SHANKER Prawn fisherman on North West coast.

SHANTEYMAN/SHANTYMAN See Chantyman.

SHEARGRINDER 15c. NFK. Sharpener of shears.

SHEARMAN One who sheared cloth or metal.

SHEATH MAKER Maker of sword cases (Sheath = scabbard).

SHELDRAKE See Scavenger. 17c. CUL.

SHEPSTER A sheep shearer.

SHINGLER 1. Rooftiler, shingles or oak being used where traditional ones were too heavy. 2.Worker in iron foundry.

SHIPMAN A mariner, master of a flat boat or barge.

SHIP'S HUSBAND Marine superintendent who has overall charge of all ships in port belonging to a firm.

SHIVER Maker of wooden pegs for barrels. A vent peg maker

SHODDY MANUFACTURER Maker of coarse woollen cloth by a process using old woollen rags which had been torn up. See Deviller, Rag Cutter, Stripper.

SHOESMITH 17c. CUL. A cobbler.

SHOE WIPER 20c. Ethiopian Court. Employed by Emperor HaileSelassie whose dogs had a habit of wetting the shoes of thosegathered at official functions.

SHOT FIRER DUR One in charge of blasting in a mine.

SHOWMAKER 17c. CUL dial. A shoemaker.

SHRAGER 16c. NFK. Trimmer or pruner of trees.

SHRIEVER 15c. NFK. Official responsible for management of law and order in village. Old English origin of the word sheriff.

SHUFFLER YKS. A young boy employed in the yards around a farmhouse.

SHUNT-MINDER Miner responsible for wagons used undergound.

SIEVEWRIGHT Maker of sieves.

SILK DRESSER Prepares silk yarn ready for weaving.

SIMISTER Seamstress.

SILKER Textile worker who sewed the ends of made up fabric. to prevent separation of layers.

SIZER 1. One who separates articles according to size. 2. One who applies size to 'dress' cloth, etc. 3. Worker in paper mill responsible for a particular stage in the paper making process.

SKEPPER/SKELPER 16c. NFK. Beehivemaker. Skelp = straw beehive.

SKIPMAKER Maker of bucket, box, cage etc, in which materials or men are drawn up and let down (mining or quarrying).

SKIPPER 1. Maker of skips, woven baskets in general use. Term varied according to area (Trugs-SSX, Slops-CUL, Swill-NFK). 2. Master of a ship.

SKIVER -(AMAZEEN/FORTUNA) One of the workers in boot and shoe manufacture who either hand finished various parts or used a specific machine which was designated Amazeen or Fortuna.

SLAPER/SLAPPER A pottery worker. Prepared lump of clay for potter by a slapping process.

SLATER Roof tiler.

SLOP-SELLER 1. Seller of baskets. Slop = Cumbrian basket, 2. Seller of ready made clothes, often ill-fitting, hence "Sloppy dresser".

SLUBBER Operator of machine preparing cotton for spinning.

SLUBBER DOFFER Removed bobbins of yarn from spindles in mills.

SMALLWARE MANUFACTURER Maker of textile articles of tape kind e.g. bindings, braids, sash cord, etc.

SMITH A worker in metal. Orig. identified by colour of metal used. Blacksmith worked in iron, Whitesmith in tin,Brownsmith in copper, Greensmith in latten, Redsmith in gold.

SMUGSMITH SSX. A smuggler.

SNUFFER MAKER 1830 Birmingham Directory. Maker of candle snuffers.

SOJOURNER CLOTHIER Itinerant dealer of cloth or clothes.

SOUTER A shoemaker, a cobbler.

SOX HAND General term for workers engaged on sock knitting frames, a Stockinger.

SPALLIER-A labourer in a tin works.

SPLITTER Worker who operated a splitting machine in various trades, one who separated material by hand, hides or skins into layers to obtain parchment and chamois leather, split reeds, willow etc., worker in stone or slate quarry.

SPOONER 15c. NFK. Maker of spoons, (A/S spoon, a chip of wood).

50

SPRAGGER Worker at mine or quarry in charge of filling and emptying wagons, tubs or carts.

SPRING-VAN MAN One employed on a spring-van, a large carriage used for removal of furniture and/or carrying passengers onexcursions.

SPURRIER See Lorimer. A spur or stirrup maker.

STAINER 1. One who coloured glass by using certain metallic pigments. 2. A dyer.

STALLMAN A collier contractor who undertakes coal hewing at a fixed rate, employing and workers himself. A Buttyman.

STAMPER Term used in several trades, from the machine or tool used by the worker, e.g. Post Office, leather finishing, sheet metal, printing.

STATESMAN Yeoman, CUL/WES.

STAY-MAKER 1. Corset maker. 2. Maker of thick strong rope used to support the masts of ships.

STENTERER Operated a cloth finishing machine.

STEP-BOY See Tiger. 19c. Young boy or man employed by public. carriage company to ride on the steps of a coach, and help passengers to mount and dismount.

STEVEDORE Stower of cargo on board ships. Dock labourer.

STILLROOM MAID Domestic. servant whose duties included waiting on and assisting the hosue-keeper in preparation of home made wines, pickles, preserves, confectionery etc.

STOCKER A skilled craftsman who made the wooden butt or stock of a shotgun or rifle.

STOCKINER Maker of stockings.

STONEMAN 1. 16c. LND. Surveyor of highways. 2. In coal mining, man employed in cutting stone drifts. 3. Quarryman

STONE-PICKER A seasonal agricultural occupation, whereby the fields were examined and all stones removed prior to crop planting. Often carried out by young children.

STONEWARDEN See Stoneman.

STONE-WORKERS Included free and rough masons, imagers, carvers, setters, wallers, paviours, tilers, quarriers, scopplers, lewers, and diggers.

STOOPER A coal-hewer (SCT).

STOWYER NFK. A net stower, a crewman on a fishing boat.

STRAVAIGER SCT. A vagabond.

STRAW-JOINER A thatcher.

STREAKER 17c. One who laid out the dead, preparing the body for burial.

STREET MASON Worked with Pavior, cutting and dressing flag stones.

STREET ORDERLY BOY 1900 Liverpool. Street cleaner.

STREETWARD Parish officer who cared for streets.

STRETCHER Employed in various textile industries in process of stretching fabrics. See Tenterer.

STRIKER Blacksmiths assistant.

STRIPPER Worker who strips off some article or product, e.g. bark from a tree, tobacco leaves, or in woollen industry the accumulation of shoddy in carding machines.

STRINGER 16c. NFK. Maker of Bow strings.

STUFFER OF BIRDS AND BEASTS Taxidermist.

STUFF WEAVER Weaver of Stuff, coarse part of flax.

SURFACE MAN 1. A labourer in charge of road repairs. 2. Worker at surface of a mine.

SWAILER/SWEALER A miller or dealer in corn.

SWEEPER OUT A mill term, applied specifically to young girl employed to keep the floor around machines clear of debris.

SWELL MAKER 16c. NFK. Maker of roughly made shallow baskets, known as swills, sweels or swulls depending on locality.

SWIN(E)YARD A pig keeper.

SWORD-PLAYER A juggler of swords.

TABLER One who keeps boarders, provides a table for them.

TACKER Dresser of cloth.

TACKLER An overlooker of power loom weavers.

TALLOW CHANDLER Maker or seller of tallow candles.

TALLY CLERK One who kept count, of arrival and despatch of goods, or work done. e.g. cargo in dock warehouses.

TALLYMAN/FELLOW A travelling draper, who gave credit and accepted payment in small instalments. 2. Tally clerk

TAN-FLAWER A Barker, one who removed bark from oak trees for the tanning of leather.

TANNER One who tanned hides and converted them into leather using various processes.

TAPISER/TAPITER Maker of Tapistry

TAPPER Innkeeper (Taphouse-inn,tavern)

TAPSTER 19C. Man employed in public. houses to serve beer from cask etc.

TAPTERE Woman in charge of the taps in a public. house or inn.

TARRIER/TERRIER-CUL, SCT. Keeper of pack of terriers.

TASKER A reaper or thresher.

TASSELER 1.14c. One who raised a nap on cloth with teasels, a prickly plant known as Fullers Thistle. Also Tozer. 2. One who made tassels for cushions, etc. 3. A nobleman.

TAVERNER An Innkeeper or Innholder.

TAWER Dresser of white leather. See Whittawer.

TEAMER/TEAMER MAN A carter or wagoner, who took care of team of horses.

TEEMER 1. In coal shipping, emptied coals out of wagons at dockside. 2. In agriculture, labourer who emptied grain from laden cart to stack. 3. In steel industry, worker who poured molten steel into moulds.

TEEAR LAD Boy employed in calico printing to stir the liquid colours continuously. (LAN)

TENTER/TENTERER An attendant, a keeper. 1. In woollen industry operator of machine which stretched cloth while drying, 2. Agricultural labourer engaged to look after animals and drive away birds after sowing.

TEXTOR A weaver.

TEYELLEYER Tailor.

THACKER A Thatcher.

THATCHER Man who covered the roofs of houses or the tops of hayricks with straw or reeds.

THIN MINER One who works in narrow seams of coal.

THIRLER/THURLER A miner who cuts out ventilation points.

THROSTLE SPINNER Skilled cotton worker who operated a power loom.

THROWSTER Textile worker attending machine which twisted together strands of yarn, cotton, silk, wool etc.

TICKNEY MAN/WOMAN An itinerant vendor of coarse common kind of earthenware. (Made at Ticknall, DBY)

TIDE GAUGER Custom house official in charge of a device which ascertained and registered the state of the tides continuously.

TIDE SURVEYOR See Tide Gauger.

TIDESMAN See Tidewaiter.

TIDEWAITER Officer who superintends the landing of goods to secure payment of duties.

TIGER 19c. A small groom or page boy in livery (uniform was traditionally a yellow waistcoat with black stripes).

TILER 15c. Bricklayer. 2. A layer of floor tiles, occasionally a roof tiler.

TIMBER MERCHANT A street match seller.(slang)

TIMBER TASTER One who examined imported wood in dockyards and ruled on its use.

TIMEKEEPER On railways , responsible for timing of trains, instructions to the driver etc. In factories, offices etc.one who booked workers in and out.

TIMES IRONER 19c. Gentlemans valet. One of whose daily duties was to iron the Times newspaper, before presentation tomaster. (Slang)

TINCTOR 14c.NFK. A dyer.

TINGLE-AIRY MAN Barrel Organ Grinder. The portable organ was slung from the man's shoulders, on which sat a small dressed monkey.

TINKER Itinerant repairer of tin vessels, kettles, pans andother metal utensils.

TINMAN One who worked with sheets of prepared tin plate forming it into various utensils on a mchine.

TIPPER 14c.CAM. One who put metal tips on the end of horns, drinking vessels etc, and possibly arrows.

TIPPLER Ale house keeper.

TIREMAN Dealer in dresses and all kinds of ornamental attire.

TIREWOMAN 18c.LND. Womens hairdresser, wigs being part of their attire. 2. Ladies maid. 3. Milliner.

TIRING BOY In textile printing one whose job was to stir the colours to prevent them clogging.(LAN).

TIXTOR 15c.NFK. Weaver (from textile.)

TODHUNTER 16c.CUL. A foxhunter, employed by the parish to keep numbers down.

TOE-RAG A corn porter, so called because of practice of binding feet to prevent being cut by hard grains. (19c. slang)

TOLLER/TOLMAN Collector of levies or tolls, at fairs, markets, roadside, mines and wharves.

TOLLIE SCT. A person who levies tolls; A turnpike keeper.

TONSOR A barber.

TOPSMAN A foreman or bailiff.

TOSIER Basket maker.

TOUCAR/TOUKER See Tucker.

TOUCH HOLER 1800. Birmingham. Worker in gun-making trade. Touchhole -small tubular hole in the breach of a firearm through which the charge is ignited.

TOWN-HUSBAND A parish officer who collected money from fathers for the upkeep of their illegitimate children.

TOWNSWAITER Officer in employ of Customs and Excise.

TOYMAN Dealer in small ornaments or articles or childrens toys.

TOZER One who tosed or teased cloth in woollen manufacture.

TRADESMAN Originally a skilled craftsman. By 18c. the term had come to include shopkeepers.

TRAMMER YKS Young pit boy. See Putter.

TRAMPLER Lawyer.

TRAPPER Young boy employed in coal mine to open and shut the air doors for the miners.

TRA(U)NTER A pedlar or hawker,carrier, carter.

TREEN MAKER Made domestic. articles of turned wood. The more highly skilled the craftsman, the more elaborately finished goods were produced. A cottage industry, by early 15c. it became the custom for young bachelors to make treen lovetokens for their sweethearts, usually a spoon (hence 'spooning' for courting).

TREENAIL MAKER Maker of long wooden pins used in ship building.

TRIPHERD Goatherd (Trip-herd of beasts) (LAN/YKS)

TRIPP(I)ER see Tripherd.

TROLLOPER A shrimp fisherman in the Wash district.

TRONAGER Official who checked local trons or weights used in assessing the tax on wool. The weights he carried were stamped with the Royal Arms and indicated his area of jurisdiction.

TROWMAN Owner of small fishing boat which has open well to keep fish alive until landed.

TROUCHMAN/TRUCHMAN 18c.SAL. Interpreter.

TRUCKMAN 19c.LND. Driver of a vehicle used for the carriage of goods, or on who loaded it with goods.

TRUNKMAKER A shopkeeper who sold trunks. Traditionally a carpenter would make the wooden box, a cordwainer the leather covering, and a lorimer the handles.

TUBBER A cooper.

TUBEDRAWER A maker of metal tubes.

TUBMAN 1. Barrister in Court of Exchequer 18c.(LON). From the tub used as a measure in excise cases. 2. Mine worker who filled containers with coal, stone, etc. 3. A Cooper or Barrelmaker.

TUCKER 1. See also Fuller, Walker. Term common in SOM and southwest England. One who thickened and cleansed woollen cloth by beating it in water. (From tuck-beat of a drum), 2. A wrapper. In needle factory one who folded and closed up packets of sewing needles by tucking in the ends of the wrapper.

TUCKER-IN A chamber maid.

TUMBESTERE see **TUMBLER**.

TUMBLER A dancer, one who leaps about, an acrobat.

TUNIST 19c.Norwich, NFK. A tuner of musical instruments.

TUPMAN Sheep farmer who bred tups or rams.

TURNER A skilled worker who used a lathe to finish or make goods and artefacts of wood, ivory,etc.

TURNCOCK One who operated valves to control the main water supply.

TURNING BOY 1.Young boy who assisted a weaver outworker in a cottage workshop, turning a bar on the loom. 2. Kitchen boy employed to turn the spit.

TURNKEY Jailer in charge of keys.

TUT-MAN A Labourer who did piece work at harvest time.

TWANGEY Tailor.

TWEENIE Victorian maid servant who worked between stairs,assisting both cook and housemaid.

TWENTYMAN Herdsman who bred twinters, two year old beasts.

TWISTERER Operator of machine which twisted several strands of yarn together to increase strength. Originally done by hand.

TWIST HAND Lace machine operator.

TWISTER and STEAMER A maker of feather boas.

UFFLER Bargeman employed occasionally in towing.

ULNAGER See Alnager.

UP AND DOWN MAN See Coal Whipper.

UPHOLDER/UPHOLDSTER Originally a maker of mattresses, quilts, hangings, anything of a padded nature including linings for coffins. In 18c. acted as chief agent in supplying furnishing for rooms and houses, often employing other craftsmen, e.g. cabinet makers, chair carvers, smiths, drapers. Hence, 1. An auctioneer or broker who 'holds up'goods for inspection. 2. Dealer in small wares or second hand articles of clothing, furniture. 3. Maker or repairer of such things.

UPHOLSTERER see Upholder.

UPRIGHT WORKER 19c.LAN. Chimney sweep.

VATMAN Skilled worker in a paper mill responsible for a particular stage in the paper making process. Term alsofound in various other trades where vats were in use.

VEGETABLE IVORY CUTTER see Ivory Nut Cutter.

VERDERER Officer responsible for the preservation of the King's Forest (from 11c.) Refers to a petty constable in some areas.

VERGE MAKER Maker of spindles for watches, clocks etc.

VERRIER 18c. A glazier, maker of glass.

VERSER A poet.

VIEWER Manager of a colliery, with offical overall authority.

VINTNER Seller of wines.

VITLER Victualler, supplier of food and drink.

WADDER NTT. Grower of the woad plant which produced a blue dye. (A/S-wad) Wadders travelled about, mainly NTT and adjacent counties and frequently appear in parish registers, Wad or woad mistakenly recorded as wood, wod, and oade

WADLER-WIFE Keeper of a register office for servants (Newcastle)

WAFERER Seller of wafers, a sort of cake or biscuit.

WAFRESTER Maker of wafers for consecration at the sacrament.

WAGGONER-Driver of heavy vehicle used in carriage of goods.

WAILER DUR Boy employed in mine to pick out slate and other impurities from coal.

WAINMAN Wagonner.

WAINWRIGHT Wagon builder.

WAIT 1.Night watchman. 2. Musician, singer.

WAKEMAN Night watchman.

WALKER See Fuller, Tucker. Term found throughout the country but most common in N. & N.W as a surname. Originally worker who cleansed and thickened woollen cloth, by process ofsubmerging it in water, and treading or walking on it.

WALKING PILLAR BOX 18c. See Bellman.

WALLER 1. Builder or repairer of dry stone walls. 2. Salt worker making coarse grained salt.

WANT CATCHER Luccombe,SOM. Mole catcher.(dial.) Also Wanter.

WAREHOUSEMAN 1. Man employed in or having charge of awarehouse. 2. Wholesale merchant.

WARPER In Textile industry , worker who set up the warp thread on a loom.

WARRENER Keeper of a warren, a piece of land appropriated for the breeding and preservation of rabbits and small game.

WASHERWOMAN Took in washing at own house or was employed in a private household for the washing of family clothes, domestic linen, etc.

WASTEMAN In DUR coal pits a worker responsible for checking old workings for gas and doing minor repairs. 2. Worker responsible for removing waste material.

WATER BADGER Mine worker responsible for baling out water from the workings when the volume was insufficient for pumping. Sometimes supplied drinking water for the pit ponies, Also called Water Leader.

WATER BAILIFF 1. An official responsible for bye-laws relating to fishing. 2. A river policeman. 3. A Customs officer in seaport towns empowered to search for contraband.

WATER GILDER 16c.NFK. Snared birds for parish.

WATER LAG Carter and seller of drinking water also Water Leader.

WATER LEADER/LEDER/LODER Carter of drinking water for sale -see Water Badger.

WATER-MAN 1. A man working on or among boats, especially a boatman who plied for hire on rivers. 2. Water Bailiff. 3. Worker in paper mill in charge of boiling raw materials.

WAY MAKER Man responsible for making roads.

WAY MAN See Way Warden.

WAY WARDEN Surveyor of highways.

WEATHER CASTER One who predicted the weather for almanacs etc.

WEAVERESS 17c.LAN. Female weaver.

WEB/STER Originally a female weaver only, but by 17c. the term applied to any weaver.

WEIGHER At docks. Responsible for weighing of unloaded cargo in the warehouses.

WELLMASTER Man responsible for adequate and clean water supply of an area.

Appendix

A Latin list of occupations

ACCUARIUS Needlemaker.
ACTUARIUS Notary.
AGELLARIUS Hayward.
AGRICOLA Farmer or husbandman.
ALLUMNUS Tanner.
ALLUTARIUS Tanner, cordwainer.
AMANUENSIS Secretary.
ANCILLA Female servant.
ARCULARIUS Carpenter, chest maker.
ARMENTARIUS Herdsman.
AUCARIUS Gooseherd.
AURIFABER/AURIFEX Goldsmith.

BAILLIVUS Bailiff, official.
BALLISTRARIUS Gunsmith.
BERCARIUS Shepherd.
BIBLIOPOLA Bookseller.
BICARIUS Bee-keeper.
BLADARIUS Corn dealer, corn-chandler.
BRASIARIUS Malster.
BRASIATOR Brewer.
BURRIARIUS Dairyman.

CALCEARIUS Shoemaker.
CALIGARIUS Bootmaker.
CARBONARIUS Collier.
CARBONATOR Charcoal burner.
CARNIFEX Butcher.
CARPENTARIUS Carpenter.
CAUPONARIUS Innkeeper.
CEROTECARIUS/CHIROTECARIUS Glover, glovemaker.
COPHINARIUS Basket-maker.
CORARIUS Currier.
CORBIO Basket-maker.
CORVERARIUS Cobbler.
CLAVIFABER Nailmaker.

COOPERTOR Roofer, thatcher.
COREATOR Currier, leather-dresser, saddler.
COUPIATOR Woodman.
CULTELLARIUS Cutler.
CULTOR Farmer, farm labourer.
CUPRIFABER Coppersmith.
CUPARIUS Cooper, barrel-maker.

DAIA/DAYA Dairymaid.
DAUBATOR/DEALBATOR Plasterer.
DOLEATOR/DOLIARIUS Cooper.

EDIFICATOR Builder, architect.
EPHIPPIARIUS Saddler.
ESCARIUS Carver.

FABER Smith.
FABER AERARIUS Coppersmith, brazier.
FABER ARGENTARIUS Silversmith.
FABER AURANTARIUS Goldsmith.
FABER CLAVARUM Keymaker, locksmith.
FABER CLAVORUM Nailmaker.
FABER FERRARIUS Blacksmith.
FABER LIGNARIUS Carpenter.
FABER ROTARIUS Wheelwright
FABRIFER/FERRIFABER Blacksmith, ironworker.
FIGULUS Potter.
FOSSATOR Digger, ditcher.
FRUMENTARIUS Corn-dealer.
FUGATOR Cattle-drover.
FUNARIUS Rope-maker.
FURNARIUS Baker .

GARBELLATOR Garbler, an inspector of spice.

GARDINARIUS Gardener.
GREGARIUS Drover, cattleman.
GROCERUS Grocer.

HAIWARDUS Hayward.
HAVENATOR Harbour master.
HORARIUS/HOROLOGIARIUS
Clockmaker.
HORTARIUS/HORTOLANUS
Gardener.
HOSARIUS Hosier.
HOSTELLARIUS Innkeeper.

INCRUSTATOR Tinker.
INGENUUS Freeholder, yeoman.

LABORARIUS - Labourer, workman.
LANARIUS Weaver of wool, wool
merchant.
LANIATOR/LANIUS Butcher.
LAPIDARIUS Stonemason.
LATERARIUS Tile maker, bricklayer.
LIGNARIUS - Joiner, cabinet-maker.
LUDIMAGISTER Schoolmaster.

MACELLARIUS Victualler,
fleshmonger.
MAGISTER Master, holder of master's
degree.
MANUBRIATOR Maker of hilts or
handles.
MARCERUS Mercer.
MARESCALLUS Marshal, farrier.
MEDICUS Physician, doctor.
MERCATOR Merchant, trader.
MERCENARIUS Mercer.
MESSARIUS Hayward, mower, farm,
bailiff.
MOLENDARIUS Miller.
MOLINARIUS Millwright.
MURARIUS/MURATOR Mason.

NAVIGATOR Boatman, lighter-man.
NOTORIUS Notary.
NUMACIUS Tollman.
NUNTIUS Messenger.
NUTRIX Nurse, wet-nurse.

OLATOR Oilman, perfumer.
OPERARIUS/ OPIFEX Craftsman,
skilled workman.
OPERATOR Workman, worker.
ORARIUS Horarius, clockmaker.
OUSTITRIX Midwife.
OVIUM PASTOR Shepherd.

PANDOXATOR Brewer.
PANNICIUS Baker.
PANNARIUS Clothier, draper.
PANNIFEX Cloth worker.
PANNITONSOR Shearman, cloth
cutter.
PAPILONARIUS Tentmaker.
PAPIROPALUS Paper-maker.
PASTELLARIUS Pieman.
PARCARIUS Park-keeper, pinder.
PECUARIUS Grazier.
PEDAGOGUS Schoolmaster.
PELLICARIUS Skinner, pelterer.
PENULARIUS Maker of hoods.
PEREGRINUS Pilgrim, traveller.
PHARMACOPOLA Apothecary.
PICTACIARIUS Cobbler.
PICTOR Painter.
PISCATOR Fisherman.
PISCENARIUS Fishmonger.
PISTOR Baker, miller.
PITEONUM Feltmaker.
PLUMBARIUS Plumber.
PONTARIUS Bridge maker or keeper.
POMARIUS Fruit-seller.
PORCARIUS Swineherd.
PORTARIUS Carrier.
POTTARIUS Potter.
PULLETARIUS Poulterer.

QUAESTOR Treasurer, paymaster.
QUARRERIUS Stone-cutter,
quarryman.
QUASSILLARIUS Pedlar.

RESTARIUS/ROPARIUS Ropemaker,
Roper.

REVELUS Pedlar.
ROTARIUS Wheelwright.

SAIO Tipstaff.
SAPONARIUS Soap-boiler, soap-maker.
SARRATOR Sawyer.
SCISSOR Tailor, barber.
SCLATARIUS Slater.
SCURIO **Stableman.**
SEPLASSARIUS Merchant, grocer.
SERIFABER Locksmith.
SPECIARIUS Spicer, grocer.
STABULARIUS Ostler, stable-man.
STATIONARIUS Bookseller, stationer.
STRUCTOR Builder, mason, bricklayer.
SUTOR Cobbler, shoemaker.
SUTOR PANNARIUS Tailor, cloth-cutter.
SUTOR VESTIARIUM Tailor

TABERNARIUS Innkeeper.
TANNARIUS/TANNATOR Tanner.
TAPETIARIUS Carpet maker, upholsterer.
TASTATOR Ale-taster.
TECTOR Plasterer, thatcher, tiler.
TEGULATOR Tiler.
TELARIUS Weaver.
TEXTOR Weaver.
THELONMANNUS Toll-collector.
THESAURIUS Treasurer.
TIBIALUS FACTOR Framework knitter, stocking-maker.
TIGNARIUS Carpenter.
TINCTOR Dyer.
TIPULATOR Seller of ale and wine.
TONELLARIUS Cooper, barrel-maker.
TONSOR Barber.
TORCHIATOR Plasterer,dauber.
TORNATOR Turner (woodwork).
TRACTOR CERVISIE Ale-drawer, tapster.

TRITULATOR Thresher.
TRONATOR Wool weigher.
TYMPANISTER Drummer

VACCARIUS Cowman.
VAGABUNDUS Vagabond
VAGUS Vagrant, tramp.
VALLETUS Esquire, yeoman, groom, journeyman.
VALITOR Assistant
VANNATARIUS/VANNATOR Winnower.
VASARIUS Keeper of crockery
VENATOR Hunter.
VERSOR Turner
VESTIARIUS Tailor, clothier.
VICTOR Cooper.
VIDULATOR Fiddler, viol-player.
VINITOR Vintner, custodian of wine.
VIRIDARIUS Verderer, park-keeper, forest officer.
VITEARIUS/VITRARIUS Glazier, glass-seller.
VITELLARIUS Victualler.

WACCARIUS Cowherd.
WANTALIUS Glover.
WARRENARIUS Game-keeper, warrener.
WESDARIUS Dealer in woad.
WIMPLERIUS Wimple maker
WUDEWARDUS Woodward.
WUDIARIUS Woodman.

XYLOPOLA Dealerin wood.
XYSTICUS Champion, a wrestler.

YCONOMUS Guardian.

ZONARIUS Girdler, belt-maker.
ZYGOSTATA Clerk of a market.

Bibliography

Cotswold Crafts, Brill, E., Batsford, 1977.

The Matchmakers, Beaver, P., Henry Melland, 1985.

The Miners, Burton, A., Andre Deutsch, 1976.

Useful Toil, Burnett, John., Penguin, 1984.

Following the Fishing, Butcher, David, Tops'l, 1987.

The Ballad and the Plough, Cameron, D.K., Futura, 1978.

The London Tradesman 1747, Campbell, R., David & Charles, 1969.

The Craftsman in Textiles, Clarke, L.J., Bell, 1968.

The Railway Navvies, Coleman, T.J., Penguin, 1968.

Occupational Costume in England, Cunningham & Lucas, A. & C. Black, 1976.

A History of Shopping, Dorothy Davies, Routledge and Kegan Paul, 1967.

Where Beards Wag All, E. Evans, Faber & Faber, 1977.

The Cooper in Liverpool, A. Grant, Industrial Archaeology Review Vol. 1:1, 1976.

City Livery Companies, Guildhall Library, 1989.

The Skilled Labourer, J.L. & B. Hammond, Longman, 1978.

The Town Labourer, J.L. & B. Hammond, Longman, 1978.

The Village Labourer, J.L. & B. Hammond, Longman, 1978.

Packmen Carriers & Packhorse Roads, D. Hey, Leics U.P., 1980.

Dictionary of Archaic Words, J.O. Halliwell, J.R. Smith, 1850.

Made in England, D. Hartley, Eyre Methuen, 1977.

The Rise and Fall of the Victorian Servant, Pamela Horn, Alan Sutton, 1990.

The Book of Trades or Library of Useful Arts, Beryl Hurley, 1811, Volumes 1-3, Wiltshire F.H.S., 1977.

Coalmining Women, Victorian Lives and Campaigns, Angela John, Cambridge U.P., 1985.

Traditional Country Craftsmen, J.G. Jemkins, Routledge and Kegan Paul, 1978.

The Census & Social Structure, R. Lawton, Cass, 1978.

The Bond of Green Withy, B. Lawrence, Cedric Chivers, 1973.

Travelling Brothers, R.A. Leeson, George Allen & Unwin, 1979 .

London Labour & the London Poor, H. Mayhew, Bohn, 1861,
Reprinted Dover, 1968.

Come Dawn Come Dusk, N. Nursell, Unwin, 1983.

To Speed the Plough, Ian Niall, Readers Union, 1978.

The Rambling Soldier, R. Palmer, Alan Sutton, 1985.

Dictionary of Historical Slang, E. Partridge, Penguin, 1972.

Women Workers and the Industrial Revolution, Ivy Pinchbeck, Virago,
1985.

A Textile Community in the Industrial Revolution, E.G. Power, Longman,
1983.

Occupational Sources: A Bibliography, Stuart Raymond, Federation of
Family History Societies, 1992.

Londoners' Occupations, Stuart Raymond, Federation of
Family History Societies, 1994.

The Local Historian's Encyclopedia, J. Richardson ed., Historical
Publications, 1977.

Labour Migration in England, A. Redford, Manchester U.P,1976.

English Industry of the Middle Ages, L.F. Salzman, Oxford, 1923.

Village Life and Labour, R. Samuel ed., Routledge and Kegan Paul, 1982.

*Miners, Quarrymen & Saltworkers, R. Samuel ed., Routledge and Kegan
Paul, 1977.*

Weavers and Outworkers in Victorian Times, Peter Searby, Longman, 1980.

'Local Industries', Various Titles and authors, Shire Publications.

Latin Word-List for Family Historians, E. Simpson, Federation of Family
History Societies, 1985.

'Peter Gurney', *Shepherd Lore,* C. S. Smith, Wiltshire Folk Life Society,
1985.

Scottish Trades and Professions, D. R. Torrance, Scottish Association of
Family History Societies, 1991.

Seventy Years of Trade Unionism 1868-1938, T.U.C., Victoria House Press,
1938.

The History of the T.U.C. 1868-1968, T.U.C., Hamlyn, 1968..

English Country Crafts, Norman Wymer, Batsford, 1946.

English Town Crafts, Norman Wymer, Batsford, 1949.